M000198237

PENGUIN CANADA

EDUCATION

Ken Osborne began his career teaching high school history in Winnipeg and then went on to teach at University of Manitoba's education faculty until he retired in 1996. He has received several awards for excellence in teaching and has written extensively on education for the popular as well as the academic press.

Understanding Canada

THE MCGILL INSTITUTE FOR the Study of Canada opened in Montreal in July 1994. Frankly, McGill is a wonderful place to study Canada. The university attracts thousands of students from across the country and internationally. Almost any class gathers French and English-speaking students from half a dozen provinces and three or four countries. McGill faculty research and comment on Canada, from its bedrock to its latest cultural fads. Their networks involve colleagues from around the world.

The Institute—MISC to its friends—was founded by the Bronfman family as a new way to make Canada, its problems and its achievements, better known. Like other academic institutes, we organize courses, sponsor research, support younger faculty and graduate students. Our public education program promotes discussion of Canadian issues. Some of our winter conferences have been broadcast across Canada. Thanks to funding from the Seagram Company, MISC brought scholars from the Canadian West and the Atlantic provinces to help students and colleagues at McGill and other Quebec universities understand regional perspectives in Canada.

If MISC has a priority, it is helping Canadians understand issues. This is tougher than it sounds. Plenty of people think democracy works best with short sound-bites, dumbed-down slogans and a telegenic smile. Yet the information revolution drowns us in the complexity of problems. Solutions, however attractive, have side-effects. In health care, patients want to understand their condition so that they can give "informed consent." Why not citizens?

As humane people in one of the world's richest countries, Canadians wonder why poverty persists. Since we or our ancestors have come from somewhere else, are there better or worse ways to manage immigration? Canadians have a host of reasons, from trade to ancestral roots, to want the world to be a peaceful, prosperous place. What are our options to help make this happen? Or as taxpayers, neighbours and especially, as proud parents, we want to understand how schools work, why they sometimes fail, and how even good schools try to become better. The answers aren't easy, but they aren't rocket science either. The Understanding Canada series was conceived by MISC as a knowledgeable, sensible, sometimes wholly unexpected journey into issues that matter to Canadians.

If sharing understanding is MISC's goal, partnership with Penguin Canada comes naturally. Generations ago, an Englishman named Carleton Lane launched a series of blue and white paperbacks dedicated to making knowledge, from the classics to astral physics, available to everyone. Styles in reading and presentation have changed, but the ideals haven't. Understanding Canada is a series designed to connect people who know with people who want to understand. Let us know if it works—and where we go next.

Desmond Morton
McGill Institute for the Study of Canada
L'Institut d'études canadiennes de McGill
3463 Peel Street, Montreal, QC H3A 1W7

EDUCATION

A Guide to the Canadian School Debate — Or, Who Wants What and Why?

Ken Osborne

PENGUIN
CANADA

A Penguin/McGill Institute Book

PENGUIN CANADA

Penguin Group (Canada), a division of Pearson Penguin Canada Inc.,
10 Alcorn Avenue, Toronto, Ontario M4V 3B2

Penguin Group (U.K.), 80 Strand, London WC2R 0RL, England
Penguin Group (U.S.), 375 Hudson Street, New York, New York 10014, U.S.A.
Penguin Group (Australia) Inc., 250 Camberwell Road, Camberwell, Victoria 3124, Australia
Penguin Group (Ireland), 25 St. Stephen's Green, Dublin 2, Ireland
Penguin Books India (P) Ltd, 11, Community Centre, Panchsheel Park,
    New Delhi – 110 017, India
Penguin Group (New Zealand), cnr Rosedale and Airborne Roads, Albany,
    Auckland 1310, New Zealand
Penguin Books (South Africa) (Pty) Ltd, 24 Sturdee Avenue, Rosebank 2196, South Africa

Penguin Group, Registered Offices: 80 Strand, London WC2R 0RL, England

First published 1999

(WEB) 10 9 8 7 6

Copyright © 1999 by Ken Osborne

All rights reserved. Without limiting the rights under copyright reserved above,
no part of this publication may be reproduced, stored in or introduced into
a retrieval system, or transmitted in any form or by any means (electronic,
mechanical, photocopying, recording or otherwise), without the prior written
permission of both the copyright owner and the above publisher of this book.

Manufactured in Canada.

NATIONAL LIBRARY OF CANADA CATALOGUING IN PUBLICATION

Osborne, Kenneth, 1936–
Education: a guide to the Canadian school debate — or, who wants what and why?

(Understanding Canada)
"A Penguin/McGill Institute book."
ISBN 0-14-028443-5

1. Education — Canada. 2. Education and state — Canada. 3. Educational change —
Canada. I. Title. II. Series: Understanding Canada (Toronto, Ont.).

LA412.082 1999   370'.971   C99-930218-3

Visit the Penguin Group (Canada) website at **www.penguin.ca**

Contents

To Janet,
who over the years has always been able to rescue me
from the bottomless depths of educational theory
and make sure that my feet are on solid ground.

Education

A Guide to the Canadian School Debate — Or, Who Wants What and Why?

Preface

THIS BOOK DOES NOT provide a blueprint for the reform of education. If it has any message at all, it is that schools are too varied and too complex to be much affected by grand plans imposed on them from on high. Successful school change comes from within the school, from what teachers do, not from the pronouncements of ministries of education. This has not, however, prevented the appearance of an endless succession of policy papers, regulations, edicts and proposals of all kinds, all aimed at shaping what schools do.

This book is not another contribution to this continuing barrage. It is intended only as a guide to the debate, an attempt to explain what the schools are actually doing, what they are being asked to do, the problems they face, and why and how some people want to change them. This is a tall order for a small book, and I have had to avoid becoming immersed in the extensive research and writing on education that has appeared in recent years, though I have certainly drawn on its findings.

The hardest part of writing this book has been deciding what to leave out, and I have left out a good deal. This book is not intended for specialists or insiders, but for people who are interested in education but do not necessarily know all that much about it.

For many Canadians, education is unknown territory. We remember our own school days, but we know very little about schools today. Just as we leave law to the lawyers and medicine to the doctors, so we leave education to the teachers. But, as we are finding out in law and medicine, education is too important to be left to the professionals. It raises questions that concern us all as citizens, whether or not we have children in school and, as citizens, we cannot afford to ignore it. More than seventy years ago, H.G. Wells uttered his now well-known judgment to the effect that civilization is a race between education and catastrophe. Some years before his death in 1946, he concluded that catastrophe was winning hands down. It has not won yet, but the race remains unfinished and we ignore education at our peril.

Though I have not advanced a personal agenda in this book, my opinions and preferences will no doubt be detectable. One of Canada's distinctive contributions to the world of politics is the idea of progressive conservatism. In education, I am best described as a progressive traditionalist, by which I mean that I believe in the value of a more or less traditional liberal education for all students, but I also believe that the so-called child-centred methods of teaching associated with progressive education are the best way to achieve it.

To use such labels, however, is to raise one of the themes of this book, which is that debate on education too often becomes an affair of labels and stereotypes, of creating false contrasts between positions that are best combined.

In writing this book I have realized, not for the first time, how much I owe to the many teachers with whom I have worked over the last thirty-five years. Their example has shown me what good teachers can accomplish, even in the most adverse circumstances. It has also reinforced my conviction that teachers are the key to educational change. No reform of education stands a chance if it does not help teachers do their work.

Though I am obviously responsible for what I have written in this book, my editor, Jackie Kaiser, has been of great assistance in helping me find ways to say it.

Part I

What Are Schools For?

CHAPTER ONE

Why Do We Have Public Schools?

THE IMPORTANCE OF SCHOOLS

WE TAKE SCHOOLS so much for granted that we sometimes forget just how important they are in our lives. The vast majority of us have been to school. The law requires parents to send their children to school. Whether we have children or not, we pay taxes to support schools. And schools, together with colleges and universities and education generally, represent, after health care, the greatest expenditure of all provincial and territorial governments.

In its concern for education, Canada is no different from any other country in today's world. Every government claims to see education as an important, often the most important, element of national policy. Developed countries see education as the key to economic prosperity. Poorer countries see it as the key to development. In today's world, to possess an efficient and effective system of education, from primary school to university, is a mark of being modern and up-to-date. Any country that refuses to take education seriously or makes the wrong educational decisions will find itself at the bottom of the world's economic league tables, or so we are told.

Even critics of the schools accept the idea of schooling. They might want to change the system, but hardly anyone wants to abolish schools. Ivan Illich's call to "deschool society" attracted some attention in the 1960s, but it is little heard these days, except perhaps from those parents who wish to educate their children at home. For

most of us, however, school is a good thing. If we want to change it
at all, we would make it more effective and more available to more
people for a longer period of time. We might not always remember
school fondly, but we realize that our children need it.

Viewed historically, our dependence on schools is relatively
new. The idea of a public school system that everyone should attend
is largely a creation of the twentieth century. Indeed, as far as high
school is concerned, it is largely a creation of the past thirty-five
years or so, for it was only in the 1960s that most Canadian students
began to complete high school.

THE ORIGINS OF PUBLIC SCHOOLING

SCHOOLS OF ONE SORT or another have a much longer history than
this, of course, but until about the last hundred years, attendance at
school was a matter of choice. No one was compelled to attend and
schools were run, not by the state, but by private institutions ranging from churches to fee-for-service, private-enterprise teachers.
Some free schools existed for boys (though hardly ever for girls) who
were thought to be especially talented, but for the most part parents,
if they so chose, and only a minority did, paid a fee to send their
children to school, most often to learn reading, writing and arithmetic, and perhaps a few other skills. The upper classes of society
expected their schools to teach various social graces, to turn boys
and, less often, girls into gentlemen and gentlewomen. Until this
century, however, the great majority of boys, and even more girls,
did not attend school, and when they did, their attendance was often
spotty. For most children and their parents, work was far more
important than school.

For most of history, children spent their lives with their parents
and other adults and learned what was expected of them from all
they saw and experienced around them. There was some teaching in
the modern sense, but it took place as needed, in the context of some
task whose relevance and importance were obvious, and was done by
whatever adult was most concerned, not by a specially trained and
appointed teacher. People learned through the family or on the job,
but not in school. Within broad limits, it was assumed that the
future would not be all that different from the present, so that what
children learned today would be useful tomorrow. In such circumstances, schools as we know them were not necessary, except in those

few instances where a small minority needed special training as scribes, priests, warriors or whatever. Some ancient societies, such as Sparta, took schooling seriously and subjected all their children to a carefully organized process of training, but they were the exception. Most left the raising of the young to the routine processes of every-day life.

Only in the nineteenth century did universal and compulsory schooling, paid for and controlled by government, become a practical possibility, largely through the coming together of three powerful forces: industrialism, nationalism and democracy.

The industrial revolution that began in the late eighteenth century transformed those societies that experienced it. The nature of work changed as factories replaced workshops. Industry began to replace agriculture as the main source of jobs. Towns and cities grew rapidly in size. The steam engine revolutionized transportation and made travel easier. Natural rhythms were replaced by those of the clock and the machine. To take only one example, the long-established custom of "Saint Monday," by which workers unofficially extended their weekend, then made up the lost work during the remainder of the week, was no longer acceptable to employers in the new industrial age.

A British wagon-maker, George Sturt, in his book, *The Wheelwright's Shop*, described the work of his sawyers in the later years of the nineteenth century. Sawyers travelled from job to job, cutting planks by hand from the trunks of felled trees. Their work was both back-breaking and highly skilled. They had to choose the right logs, decide how to cut them and then use their two-handed saws over a saw-pit, with the master sawyer on top of the log and his helper underneath. Sturt was full of praise for their strength and skill but less impressed by their work habits. Working in pairs and usually renting rooms in local pubs as they travelled from work site to work site, the slightest quarrel or delay would send one or the other of them back to the pub for a drink. According to Sturt, it could be Thursday before they got themselves organized enough to begin the week's work.

The new industrial employers, with their heavy investments in machinery and their need to make a regular profit, found such workers unreliable and welcomed inventions like the power-driven circular saw, with its ability to turn out a guaranteed product on demand. Machines worked at a steady pace, did not get tired or answer back, and did what they were told. They were more reliable and more efficient than such fiercely independent men as Sturt's sawyers.

As strange as it might sound today, many workers before the coming of the industrial revolution shared the sawyers' attitude towards work. In the words of one recent historian, the pre-industrial worker "lived for the day, gave no thought to the morrow, spent much of his meagre pittance in the local inn or alehouse, caroused the Saturday of pay, the sabbath Sunday, and 'Holy Monday' as well, dragged himself reluctantly back to work Tuesday, warmed to the task Wednesday and laboured furiously Thursday and Friday to finish in time for the long weekend."[1]

This was unacceptable in the new industrial factories, which turned workers into machine-minders who did what they were told and not what they pleased. It was not easy to turn men and women who were used to working more or less at their own speed on the land or in small workshops into people who would work at the speed of machines that they did not themselves control. In this process of changing long-established work habits, schools were seen as having a useful part to play. Employers wanted reliable, productive and clock-based work habits from their workers and saw in schools a way to instill them. Schools would train children to tell the time, to run their lives by the clock, to work hard even at tasks they saw no point in, to obey orders and generally to accept what life offered them without complaint.

As well as being a time of industrial revolution, the nineteenth century also saw the rise of nationalism as a powerful political force. The idea was widely accepted that people could be divided into nations, largely on the basis of language and culture, and that each nation was entitled to its own country, with its own territory and government. As nationalists quickly found out, however, nations are not so much born as made. For example, in countries such as Italy and France, many people did not know the national language, but instead spoke their own local languages. They identified with their own local region, not with their country as a whole. Thus, national citizens had to be made, and in this process schools were assigned an important role. It was in school that children learned the national language, read the national stories, sang the national songs, studied the national history and generally became patriotic citizens, proud of their own country and suspicious of all others.

There was another side to nationalism, however. It could be a force for democracy. Nationalists believed that the nation belonged to its people, not a king or emperor, and that the people had the right to a voice in their country's affairs. In its democratic version, nationalism gave rise to the belief that citizens were entitled to rights, not the least of which was the right to vote. This made education important. Liberals and conservatives alike agreed that if working men and, eventually, women, were to be allowed to vote and to take part in public affairs, then they should at least be able to do so intelligently. Education was necessary if democratic citizenship was to be a reality. Even more, education was a fundamental right of citizenship.

These three forces—industrialism, nationalism and democracy—created a climate of opinion that by the end of the nineteenth century made compulsory public schooling a reality. Conservatives saw schools as a force for social stability, a way of teaching people to accept their place in the world. Liberals saw them as a basic human right, a way of preparing people for peaceful change and progress. Nationalists saw them as a way of creating a sense of national identity and patriotism. Socialists saw them as offering workers a chance to get an education and so hasten the day when they would be able to seize political power.

Some people opposed compulsory public schooling. Minorities saw the new national schools as a threat to their culture and identity. Churches did not believe that education could be separated from religion and resisted what they saw as an attack on their own well-established schools. Some parents thought they could educate their children better than any school could. And some liberals and socialists worried that making education a state responsibility was giving too much power to government and that public schools would teach nothing but political propaganda.

DEMOCRATIC PROGRESS OR SOCIAL CONTROL?

MOST PEOPLE SEE THE creation of the free public schooling as a sign of enlightened progress and the advance of democracy. They believe that education is the basis of individual success and social well-being. In the 1960s, however, another interpretation began to gain ground. It saw schooling as a form of "social control" by which those in power successfully maintained their position by teaching children that the world was in the best shape it could be in, so there was no point in trying to change it. It is certainly not difficult to find examples of exactly this kind of thinking among the school promoters of the nineteenth and early twentieth centuries. The clearest example of it in Canada is the way in which schools were set up for First Nations children with the intent of destroying their culture, right down to its roots in language and heritage, and assimilating them into white society.

This "social control" view of schooling is too simplistic. Many of the groups that were to be "controlled" through schooling in fact wanted to go to school. They were not dupes, unaware of what was intended to happen to them. They believed they could benefit from education. Trade unionists, feminists, socialists and social reformers of all kinds saw in education a possible vehicle for social change. For them, to be educated meant being able to understand how the world worked and how it might be changed. Some of them even saw education as a step towards revolution. Free education for all children in public schools was even a demand in the Communist Manifesto of 1848.

In reality, schools have been both a step towards democracy and a form of social control. Some people have used the schools to block social change; others have used them to advance it. Some people have benefitted more from education than others. Schools have not been pure and simple agents of social progress, but neither have they been instruments of ruling-class domination. They are arenas in which competing social agendas struggle to make themselves felt.

Schools and schooling are, in the broadest sense of the term, political. This is certainly true in parts of the world where political parties have well-worked-out educational programs that are treated as part of the broader social policy. It is much less common in Canada, where, except for some routine ideas about equality of opportunity, meeting students' needs and the like, political parties have for the most part steered clear of education policy, treating it largely as an administrative matter best left to the professionals. If nothing else, the contemporary debate on schools and schooling will have done a useful service if it gives education the political importance it deserves and so badly needs.

All of which raises the question that underlies much of our current debate: What are schools for?

SCHOOLING FOR CITIZENSHIP

FOR MOST OF THEIR history, schools existed to teach particular skills, ranging from reading and writing through learning a second or third language, such as Latin, to preparing young men for university studies. They aimed to introduce students to the world of knowledge so that they would in due course become wise and learned, or at least have a few basic academic skills. All this changed in the late nineteenth and early twentieth centuries when governments decided to erect compulsory, universal, public school systems, which were intended above all to turn children into useful citizens. As the superintendent of Winnipeg schools noted in 1913, the traditional educational goals of what he called "culture and discipline"—by which he meant mental and intellectual discipline—were no longer enough. In the new world of industry, nationalism and democracy, education had also to produce in children a sense of civic duty, a patriotic spirit, good health and preparation for jobs. In other words, schools existed to train citizens.

This fundamental shift of approach was the working out in education of the consequences of the forces of nationalism, industrialism and democracy that dominated Western Europe and North America during the nineteenth century. In the case of Canada, especially in the West and to some extent Ontario, widespread concern about the effects of immigration gave the shift a special urgency. The large numbers of immigrants from Central and Eastern Europe had to be Canadianized, which meant that they had to learn English, to identify with Canada's British heritage, to understand the Canadian political process since they would sooner or later get the right to vote, to master the three R's and generally to become assimilated into mainstream Canadian society.

On the positive side, citizenship was based on the conviction that Canada had to develop a national spirit so that Canadians would see themselves as Canadians and would put the good of Canada as a whole above the good of any particular group or region. On the negative side, this usually meant the assimilation of religious and linguistic minorities and of Native Canadians to a narrow view of what it meant to be Canadian. In Quebec, it was seen as a threat to the French language and to Quebec culture.

At the same time, citizenship also carried within it some very different possibilities. If it threatened forced uniformity in a narrowly defined Canadian nationality, it also offered the promise of democracy, respect for rights and the chance to participate in public life regardless of personal background. Thus, women successfully won citizenship rights, including the right to vote and to hold public office and to be recognized as persons within the meaning of the Constitution. So did workers when they won the right to organize, to bargain and to strike.

Definitions of citizenship over the years became more generous and inclusive. Assimilation gave way to multiculturalism; unilingualism to bilingualism; uniformity to diversity. As ideas of citizenship changed over time, so did approaches to citizenship education. By the 1970s, Canadian citizenship education had come to consist of six principal elements. It aimed to give students: (1) a sense of identity as Canadians but also as citizens of the world; (2) an awareness of and respect for human rights; (3) an acceptance of the responsibilities and obligations of citizenship; (4) a reflective commitment to broad social values; (5) the capacity to participate in public life; and (6) the ability to think about and act intelligently on the implications of the preceding elements.

TWO VIEWS OF TEACHING

FOR THE SCHOOLS, THE problem became how to turn the goal of citizenship into reality. In very broad terms, there were two contrasting theories. The older and more traditional view of teaching saw it as the imparting of necessary information, skills and values to children. The favourite images were those of filling an empty jug, writing on a clean slate or processing raw material. Students came to school and had their minds filled by their teachers, using the official curriculum and textbooks, and then went on their way. It was a view that saw the teacher as the giver of knowledge and the student as its more or less passive recipient. Its critics sometimes called it the "drill and kill" approach to teaching.

The second approach was the opposite of the first. Its supporters, including many teachers, rejected the view of students as empty jugs or clean slates, as raw material waiting to be processed. They saw students as individual human beings who brought with them to school a wealth of experience, knowledge and ideas, and they believed that effective teaching must take this into account. They dismissed the outside-in approach to teaching in favour of working with what students already knew and extending and refining it. They insisted that students had to be active, both physically and mentally, that learning was not just remembering and repeating but doing and working and thinking. They argued that the traditional approach was not even effective in its own terms, since students quickly forgot most of what they had been taught.

As so often in education, the debate became an exchange of stereotypes and slogans, but it marked and continues to mark a continuing tension in education, and one that never fails to rouse public and parental concern, since it raises fundamental questions of standards and effectiveness. Today it is seen in the conflict between so-called progressive, child-centred methods and what is now called direct instruction and whole-class teaching.

REFERENCES

1. David S. Landes. *The Unbound Prometheus: Technological Change, 1750 to the Present*. Cambridge: Cambridge University Press, 1969, p. 59.

CHAPTER TWO

The Goals of Education

LOOKING BACK TO THE SIXTIES

CRITICS OF TODAY'S SCHOOLS sometimes say that the rot set in in the 1960s when standards were abandoned, schools became permissive, and teachers adopted a philosophy of "anything goes." In the 1960s, schools were increasingly seen as conformist and authoritarian, teaching irrelevant and outdated curricula to bored and apathetic students. An American writer, Charles Silberman, wrote a best-selling critique of schools, *Crisis in the Classroom*, accusing them of "mindlessness" which he saw manifested in overly rigid curricula, traditional teaching methods and a general failure to meet students' needs. In Canada, the best-known example of this argument is probably Ontario's 1968 Hall-Dennis Report, which criticized schools for what it described as their "inflexible programs, outdated curricula, unrealistic regulations, regimented organization, and mistaken aims of education." It proposed instead a school system that would be organized, not around fixed curricula, examinations and external controls, but around programs tailored to individual students' needs.

The language of the report is so foreign to today's educational concerns that it is worth quoting, if only to remind us of a world we have largely forgotten:

> The lock-step structure of past times must give
> way to a system in which the child will progress

from year to year throughout the school system
without the hazards and frustrations of failure. His
natural curiosity and initiative must be recognized
and developed. New methods of assessment and
promotion must be devised. The curriculum must
provide a greater array of learning experiences
than heretofore. Classes must be more mobile,
within and beyond the local environment, and the
rigid position of education must yield to a flexibility capable of meeting new needs. These and other
innovations will be aimed at developing in the
child a sense of personal achievement and responsibility commensurate with his age and ability,
to the end that going to school will be a pleasant
growing experience, and that as he enters and
passes through adolescence he will do so without
any sudden or traumatic change and without a
sense of alienation from society.[1]

The Hall-Dennis Report was typical of a mood that was sweeping the country by the end of the 1960s. Across Canada, schools
changed with remarkable speed: dress codes were relaxed, compulsory study halls disappeared and students were given free periods,
external examinations were eliminated, course electives multiplied,
teacher-student relations became more egalitarian.

By the 1990s all this had begun to change. What in the 1960s
had been seen as necessary and long-overdue reforms were now
rejected as permissive nonsense. What had then been rejected as
dead traditionalism was now praised as evidence of high standards.
The crisis in the classroom was now identified as precisely the
flexibility that the 1960s had welcomed. In open-area schools, the
walls went up. Course electives were reduced. External examinations were brought back. The amount of time spent in the classroom was increased. Teachers were told to return to more
traditional methods of teaching. Schools were urged to go back to
the basics—or forward to the basics, as some sceptics suggested—
unconvinced that schools had ever properly taught the basics
in the first place. So-called child-centred teaching became the target of vehement criticism. The Hall-Dennis report, which in its
day had been the shining star of educational reform, now was

painted as at best woolly-minded idealism and at worst reckless irresponsibility.

THE NEEDS OF STUDENTS
OR THE NEEDS OF SOCIETY?

THE DEBATE IS THE latest manifestation of a long-standing educational problem: Should schools serve the needs of students or the needs of society, and who decides just what these needs are? If the answer is both, then where does one strike the balance between them? Most ministries of education seem to think they are one and the same, and obviously in some ways they are. When students learn to read and write, to understand the obligations of citizenship, to obtain the skills necessary to hold down a job and so on, both they and society benefit. However, the tension that exists between the needs of society and the needs of the individual student is not always so easily resolved.

Suppose, for example, that society needs all Canadians to know and understand their country's history—which at present about half the ministries of education in the country do not appear to believe—how does one persuade sceptical grade eleven or twelve students that this is something they also need? As one Newfoundland student who intended to join the police force told an investigator in the 1980s, "I'm not going to think about how Cabot discovered Newfoundland when I'm doing my job."

To take another example, some people now argue that Canada "needs" only a certain proportion of its young people to attend university, while others should attend community college, enter apprenticeship programs or go straight into the workforce. The Harris government in Ontario has suggested that students who do attend university should be steered into certain programs and away from others, such as sociology or geography. In the same way, a Manitoba task force has proposed that postsecondary education should be geared towards meeting the province's economic needs and away from the arts and the humanities.

If these proposals become reality, high schools will have to sort their students into programs that prepare them for their intended careers, but this could well conflict with the desire of parents to see their children get the best education possible. In the 1960s the Manitoba Department of Education decided to depart from its established pattern of offering one high school program, the "matriculation" course, to the great majority of students. Instead a new university-entrance program was designed, intended for roughly the top thirty percent of students, with a general program for the so-called average students, and a remedial program for the remainder. Parents and students, however, quickly caught on and overwhelmingly demanded that their children take the "best" program on offer, which they defined as the one that provided students with the most choices at the end of high school. As a result most students signed up for the university-entrance program, with the general course quickly earning a reputation as a dumping ground. The needs of society, at least as defined by the Manitoba Department of Education, came into direct conflict with the needs of students—and lost.

Most teachers think first of their students, not of society. They define their jobs as meeting the needs of their students. They get their greatest job satisfaction from seeing their students succeed. The very first article of the code of professional practice of the Manitoba Teachers' Society reads: "A teacher's first professional responsibility is to his or her students." It does not say to follow the curriculum, or to obey the directives of the department of education, or even to meet the needs of society, but to respond to students, and in this it is typical of similar codes right across the country. If taken literally it means that a teacher should scrap the curriculum if it does not seem appropriate or helpful for a particular student.

Teachers see themselves, not as servants of the government or as agents of society, but as nurturers of children. This is why most of them go into teaching in the first place: not to change the world or even to pursue their subject, but to work with children. Their measure of success is not that they made a child a good Canadian, or covered the year's work, or were declared teacher of the year, or even that they helped Canadian students outperform the Japanese on an international math test, but that they helped a student get to university or to pass grade ten English, when all the predictions were that he or she would fail.

When I was a student teacher in England, I was assigned to teach a collection of short stories to a class of twelve-year-olds, only to find that I could not do it. The stories had been written in the early 1900s and conveyed a set of racist assumptions about the "white man's burden" and the glories of the British Empire. I simply abandoned them and found an assortment of stories that were less objectionable and also more interesting to my students, who still learned about English usage, story writing, and grammar, but embodied in a better content.

Years later in Canada I was consulted by a frustrated student teacher who had to teach an unruly group of grade seven students. Because they did not like most schoolwork, the students had been given an alternative curriculum that dealt with the history of Manitoba. The school saw these students as "non-academic" and assumed they would find something local and close at hand more interesting than the official program of Greek and Roman history. Unfortunately the idea did not work, and when I watched the class in action, I felt that the student teacher had been stuck with an impossible job. My not-very-helpful advice was that he should teach something completely different that would at least hold students' attention while also serving some educational purpose. In fact, it seemed to me that the students would find ancient Greece and Rome, with their myths, battles, gladiators and assorted blood and thunder, far more interesting than almost anything to do with the local area. But because they were judged to be non-academic, and because they were certainly an unruly bunch, the school had decided that ancient history was too "academic" for them. If they had been my class, I would have junked the local-history curriculum and taught ancient Greece and Rome instead.

Teachers often face problems like this, but they are ignored by those school critics now calling for much tighter control over what teachers actually teach and for much stricter enforcement of a system-wide curriculum. This is why so many teachers are uneasy with the current calls for standards, accountability, effectiveness and all the other buzzwords of contemporary school reform. They are not lazy or irresponsible. They fear that such demands will penalize students by making curricula even more boring than they already are in many students' eyes, and so making teaching them more difficult, while also ignoring the problems that students so often bring to school with them and that demand attention before any kind of academic teaching can begin.

The teachers' objection is that the agenda of today's school reformers simply ignores the social reality in which all too many students find themselves, whereby their first priority is not so much algebra or geography but a square meal and personal safety. Teachers, however, speak from a script that is written in terms of students' needs. Today's reformers, by contrast, are driven by what they see as the needs of society, and particularly of the need to guarantee Canada's continuing economic prosperity in an age of increasing global competition.

Wherever one stands in this debate, whether one believes that schools exist to meet the needs of students, or that schools should above all serve the needs of society, or, more likely, that some appropriate balance should be struck between the two, it is important to realize that this tension underlies much of today's concern about schools. It is also important to realize there are rarely any easy answers to the questions that arise.

There is no way of deciding in some objective way just what the needs of students and society are and trying to balance one against the other. The idea of need is much more complicated than it looks, at least in education. It is easy to say that someone who is hungry needs a good meal, but that is very different from deciding that a student "needs" Latin or chemistry. And even when we say that a hungry person needs a square meal, we can still disagree over just what that meal should contain.

In my air force days I was nagged by a sergeant who regularly told me that I needed a haircut, but, as I used to tell him, the need was really his, not mine. I was perfectly comfortable with the state of my hair and felt no personal need to get it cut at all. So when we hear talk of the needs of society, we have to ask ourselves who is defining those needs. In whose interest is it to use the schools to make students more entrepreneurial, competitive and adaptable, for instance? Why should education policy be directed so single-mindedly at job training and economic prosperity? And even if it should be, is not a broad liberal education, as more or less traditionally understood, still the best preparation for economic, as for other, success?

EDUCATION AND THE ECONOMY

TODAY, EDUCATION IN ALL parts of Canada is being turned into an instrument of economic policy. An Ontario report in 1987 described education as "the paramount ingredient for competitive success in the world economy" and as crucial "for our very survival as an economically competitive society."[2] It is a view that now dominates education policy. We are told that Canada's material prosperity, and even its very survival, depends upon competing with other countries for a bigger slice of the global economic pie. Historically, it is pointed out,

Canada became prosperous by exporting its raw materials and importing finished goods and by protecting a basic level of heavy industry. Most jobs did not need much education, and there were plenty of jobs for whoever needed them.

But conditions have changed. Canada can no longer rely on the export of raw materials, nor can it compete with the lower cost of manufacturing found in the developing countries of the world. Moreover, the ability of capital to move quickly around the world and of transnational corporations to locate production where they please, combined with the move towards freer trade, mean that the old ways of doing things are no longer adequate. From now on Canadians' prosperity and standard of living will increasingly depend on high-tech, knowledge-based jobs, on the application of high levels of skill, and a willingness to adapt and adjust to the changes of the global economy. The future, therefore, depends on education, on a skilled and flexible workforce, comfortable with sophisticated technology and eager to face uncertainty and change, ready to define risk as challenge and opportunity.

Ministries of education take this argument very seriously. Throughout the 1990s they have been telling schools that they should concentrate on preparing students for the new global economy. They should form close links with business. They should emphasize computer skills, mathematics and science. They should concentrate, not on literature, but on literacy. They should teach the skills and habits needed in the workplace of the future: teamwork, problem-solving, decision-making, and so on. And they should teach students that the world does not owe them a living and that they must learn to be entrepreneurial, adaptable and competitive, ready and able to create their own jobs when they lose the jobs they have.

The argument ignores the reality that the greatest increase in jobs today is occurring not in high-tech industry but in the unskilled and semi-skilled, low-wage, service sector. It also ignores the reality that technology is not taking us into a paradise where everyone will be highly skilled and educated, happily changing jobs at regular intervals and, when they cannot find a job, confidently creating their own. Rather, it is taking us into a world where a minority of people will have challenging, rewarding and well-paid work, but where the majority will find themselves de-skilled and engaged in work, often part-time, that has already been programmed for them.

Above all, the argument expects far more from the schools than they can possibly deliver. Even if the schools were miraculously able to turn all students into highly skilled and entrepreneurial workers, this would not in the least guarantee that there would be jobs for them to enjoy. Education, on its own, does not create jobs. That depends on a coherent industrial strategy, on economic policy, on the encouragement of research and development, and on a host of other policies, as well as sheer luck, that go far beyond education. In their rush to reshape schooling to serve economic goals, governments are avoiding the tough decisions upon which real economic development depends. To assume that school reform as currently conceived is the key to economic development is akin to applying a Band-Aid to heal a heart attack.

Even worse, it fatally distorts what ought to be the real purposes of schooling. To prepare the young for the world of work is only one of the functions of schooling. The others are to prepare students for their role as citizens and to lay the foundations that will enable them to live rich and fulfilling lives as individual men and women.

A RETURN TO CITIZENSHIP

AS FAR AS CITIZENSHIP IS concerned, schools should introduce students to the widest possible range of knowledge and activities that they might not otherwise encounter and help them think about the "big questions" of life, however simply. They should also make it possible for children to find and develop their special talents and interests—all with the aim of giving them a foundation upon which they can make as much of their lives as possible. This is why music and art, physical education and sport, literature and drama, for example, can never be regarded as "frills."

To use history as an example, where but in school will students learn about the world of the Maya, the Inca and the Aztecs, or the African kingdoms of Ghana, Mali, Zimbabwe and Songhay? Where but in school will they meet Nellie McClung or Marguerite Bourgeois, Joan of Arc or Rosa Luxemburg, or learn of the vital role that generations of unremembered First Nations women played in the western Canadian fur trade? This kind of encounter enriches students' lives, and makes them less self-centred by connecting them with other people in other times and places.

We need to return to the tradition that saw citizenship as the central task of the public schools. Not the citizenship of intolerant patriots busily rooting out dissent and unorthodoxy, but the free and thoughtful citizenship whose roots lie in traditional Native values of discussion and consensus, in ancient Athens, in the civic humanism of the Italian Renaissance, in the ideals of the American and French revolutions, and in the democratic movements of the nineteenth and twentieth centuries. It is a vision that has had its blind spots, most notably in its treatment of women and of minorities, but it is a vision that contains the potential for its own correction. It sees citizenship as the difficult art of balancing personal freedom with social responsibility. It insists on the importance of rights, but also on the performance of duties. Its sees citizenship not as something static and changeless, but as the subject of debate, struggle and development.

Nor is the call to make citizenship the central purpose of education a call to return to the old narrow view of citizenship that defined it in terms of assimilation to a prescribed vision of Anglo-Canadian society. It is a call to see that in any society that claims to be democratic, education for citizenship is crucial. Democracy depends on the commitment and participation of its citizens. Like a muscle, if it is not exercised, it withers away. It requires that citizens be well-informed, thoughtful, tolerant and interested in public affairs, and this in turn demands a level of knowledge and skills, as well as a commitment to values, that requires education. Democratic citizenship is not something we are born with; it is something we learn, and we learn much of it in our schools.

In the Canadian context, citizenship, properly understood, must be a particular priority. Canada is a diverse country, with strong regional differences, with a commitment to multiculturalism, all wrapped in a federal structure that sometimes makes it difficult to hold the country together, and facing powerful influences from the United States. As John Ralston Saul has argued in his *Reflections of a Siamese Twin*, Canada is not a conventional nation-state along the lines of France, Britain or the United States, and many of our difficulties come from our attempts to live as though we were one. Canada's existence requires special qualities in its citizens: acceptance of diversity, a willingness to live with ambiguity, an understanding of the nature of the country and a familiarity with its history and, not least, the ability to enter into the continuing debate that characterizes Canadian public life. These qualities can and should be nurtured in the schools, although most ministries of education in Canada these days seem willing to cast them aside. In the brave new world of the global future, it seems, we will be neither individual men and women seeking to make the best of our lives, nor citizens engaged with others in a common enterprise, but only workers and consumers, fodder for the technological future.

A SCHOOL'S NEED FOR
AN EDUCATIONAL PHILOSOPHY

WHEN I ARRIVED IN WINNIPEG in 1961 to teach in a local high school, I was welcomed by the principal, presented with my timetable and given to understand that as a professional teacher it was now my task to get on with the job. I was given no curriculum, no statement of philosophy, no orientation to the school as a whole—nothing beyond the authorized textbooks and a friendly greeting. This was understandable, since I knew, as did my principal, that my job was to get as many students as possible through the provincial examinations, while playing some part in the general life of the school. Both the principal and I understood what my job was. There was no need to talk about it.

Today, however, things are not so clear. Thirty years ago, examinations, whether good or bad, at least provided us with a sense of purpose. They were, so to speak, the enemy, and teachers and students worked together to defeat them. That, at least, was how I explained things to my students. With the disappearance of examinations, life became more complicated. If I was now supposed to evaluate my students, what should I evaluate them for? And how did what I was doing in my classroom compare with what other teachers were doing in theirs? How did a school ensure that its teachers were all working towards the same goals?

This loss of a sense of common purpose was made worse by the willingness of education ministries and other agencies to give schools new tasks that were more social than educational, with the result that teachers often took on the job of being social workers and therapists.

In these circumstances, a clear definition of educational goals, which teachers, parents and students can all accept, is important. School policies are often established to deal with specific problems, such as truancy, lateness, smoking, bullying, reporting to parents, and so forth. They work on their own terms, but often do not add up to a coherent and consistent vision of where a school is or ought to be heading. Sometimes they fly in the face of the very goals that a school claims are important. Here, for example, are the categories used on an elementary school report card in western Canada: gets along with others; uses time to good advantage; completes assignments; works quietly and independently; listens well; dependable; produces neat work; takes criticism and disappointment well.

Taken together, these categories suggest that the task of the student is to sit down, shut up, follow instructions and work. To some extent, this is reasonable, for students have to learn to follow instructions and complete assigned tasks. There is another aspect of education, however, which this report card did not deal with at all. Where are the categories that describe such qualities as creativity, originality, critical thinking and initiative? These were all qualities the school professed to value, but its report card failed to mention them. The school suffered from not having a clear statement of educational philosophy, which could be used to check that what it was actually doing in practice matched its theory.

Educational philosophy matters. Like any other institution, a school works better when it operates on the basis of a set of shared beliefs. When one of my children years ago got his first part-time job in a fast-food restaurant, his first hours on the job were occupied in studying the company's mission statement, its rules for treating customers, its work expectations and its regulations about general conduct. He had to become a member of the team. This rarely happens in schools, where teachers new to a staff simply report in, pick up their teaching assignments and get on with the job in any way they see fit. Research into what makes some schools particularly effective shows that a key factor in their success is that they have a clear philosophy that all teachers accept and use as a basis for their teaching, and that all school policies are consistent with it. The result is that students do not have to be preached at; they learn what is expected of them from everything they meet in their school. This is not especially surprising. Perhaps the greatest strength of private schools is that they each embody a set of shared values and beliefs that shape every aspect of school life.

In public schools, things are more complicated. The wide diversity of parents, teachers and students makes it more difficult to achieve agreement on school priorities and policies. Moreover, a public school cannot exclude students who do not fit in with its way of doing things. Nor, in the usual run of events, do public schools enjoy the level of parental involvement and support enjoyed by private schools. And the turnover of teachers makes it difficult to maintain any consistent philosophy among the staff, as some teachers move on and others move in, often on the basis of seniority and service or of contractual obligations, not on the basis of a shared educational philosophy.

We need more thorough public discussion of educational goals and purposes, discussion that goes far beyond the slogans that dominate debate today. As things stand, a vacuum exists as far as the purposes of schooling are concerned, with the result that those who wish to direct schools to serve economic goals are winning their case more or less by default. While it is obviously important for schools to prepare students for jobs, other goals remain important. Indeed, it might be that achieving them will turn out to be the best career preparation anyway. Here, for example, are the educational goals set out by the government's department of education in England some years ago:

- to help pupils to develop lively, enquiring minds, the ability to question and argue rationally and to apply themselves to tasks and physical skills;
- to help pupils to acquire knowledge and skills relevant to adult life and employment in a fast-changing world;
- to help pupils to use language and numbers effectively;
- to instill respect for religious and moral values, and tolerance of other races, religions and ways of life;
- to help pupils understand the world in which they live, and the interdependence of individuals, groups and nations;
- to help pupils to appreciate human achievements and aspirations.[3]

More simply, the 1988 British Columbia Royal Commission on Education spoke of four purposes of schooling, which it described as: the cultivation of mind, preparation for vocational life, moral and civic development, and individual development. In Ontario, the 1994 Royal Commission on Learning defined three purposes of schooling. The first was to ensure for all students high levels of "literacies: building on basic reading, writing, and problem-solving skills to ever-increasing stages, as well as ever-deepening degrees of understanding across a variety of subject areas." The second was the development in students of a wish to continue learning and the ability and commitment to do so. The third was the preparation of students for responsible citizenship, including the development of "basic moral values, such as a sense of caring and compassion, respect for the human person and anti-racism, a commitment to peace and non-violence, honesty and justice."[4]

THE TWELVE C'S

ALL SUCH STATEMENTS ARE obviously very general and they can easily be lost sight of in the daily bustle of the classroom. What we need is some sort of key that will enable us to apply an educational philosophy to the realities around us in a manageable way, in the manner of an architectural guidebook that helps us spot the significant features of a building without getting lost in a mass of unfamiliar detail. In this spirit, I have found useful the following list of what I call the Twelve C's, using the letter *C* not for any deep reason, but simply as a convenient aid to memory so that the list can be easily applied in daily classroom use.

The first C is *Canadian* and it asks whether their schooling teaches students enough about Canada—its history and geography, its artistic, scientific and other achievements, and its current problems—to help them understand and to participate in the continuing debate that is so fundamentally Canadian: What kind of country are we and what kind of country do we want to be?

The second C stands for *cosmopolitan*, in the traditional sense of the word. It asks whether their schooling teaches students that they are citizens not only of Canada, but of the world. Do they think not only of their own country or their own group, but also of the world as a whole?

The third C stands for *communication*, and asks whether schooling gives sufficient emphasis to teaching students to communicate effectively in all the different forms that communication can take: speech, writing, numeracy, graphics and so on.

Since the ability to communicate cannot be separated from the content to be communicated, the fourth C stands for *content*. Does schooling give students adequate command of a broad body of subject matter, representing the humanities and social sciences, mathematics and science, the expressive arts and so on?

This content, however, must be more than a collection of quiz-show knowledge. It must stimulate thought and questioning. It must be coupled with the fifth C, which is *curiosity*, the desire to inquire, to find out, to keep on learning.

This leads to the sixth C, which stands for *critical*. It asks whether schooling teaches students to think critically, and whether teachers approach knowledge not as sacred dogma, but as an invitation to inquiry and reflection, because acquiring knowledge but never using it is of little benefit since it does not lead one to think and to improve one's reasoning powers.

Criticism, however, can be little more than a reactive process, and education should involve more than teaching one to simply respond to the ideas of others. Therefore, the seventh C represents *creativity*, which is something all people possess in one form or another. It draws attention to the extent to which schooling actively seeks to foster creativity in students, not only in the arts but in all subjects.

Creativity does not exist in a vacuum. It draws its inspiration from what has been called the "great conversation," the continuing dialogue that has existed for centuries in all civilizations about the meaning and nature of life. Thus, the eighth C stands for *civilization*. It asks whether schooling seeks to convey to students an adequate understanding of the civilizations (in the plural) of which they are both the heirs and the trustees for the future.

Civilization is a collective, co-operative enterprise, and this leads to the ninth C, *community*. It raises the question of whether and to what extent schooling seeks to prepare students to become informed, participating and involved members in their various communities: local, national and global.

This in turn leads to the tenth C, which stands for *concern*, and asks whether and how schooling creates in students a sense of concern, and a readiness to act on that concern, both for other people and for the environment that makes life possible.

None of this is possible without the eleventh C, which stands for *character*. Years ago the development of character was seen as a key purpose of education. It represents the willingness to do what is right, to act morally, to follow one's conscience, to balance one's own concerns against the rights of other people. It is not a word that is much used today; we need to revive it.

Finally, the twelfth C stands for *competence*. It asks how effective schooling is in playing its part in preparing students to be effective and competent citizens, workers and human beings. A British educator, F.W. Sanderson, headmaster of Oundle School and a man H.G. Wells once described as the greatest man he had ever met—no small tribute in view of Wells's acquaintance with the great and famous of his day—wrote of his teaching in the 1920s: "We will first of all transform the life of the school, then the boys, grown into men—and girls from their schools, grown into women—whom their schools have enlisted into this service, will transform the life of the nation and of the whole world."[5] That conveys the essence of competence, as the word is intended here.

All this may seem overly ambitious, but not when it is spread out over twelve years of schooling. The list is not intended to be applied to one particular lesson but to the whole range of a school's activities. The Twelve C's represent the whole of schooling. If attained, they will equip any student for success. Equally important, they will contribute to the shaping of the kind of community in which individual success derives from and contributes to social purposes. More specifically, they can help us focus on just what it is that we expect from our schools in a way that is concrete enough to make sense in the classroom. The Twelve C's are a checklist of the kind that pilots run through before they fly a plane. They are intended to help teachers in their planning and parents in their examination of what their children learn.

In the words of the 1993 Newfoundland Royal Commission on Education, "to strengthen the links between each part of the system, parents, teachers, administrators, and policy-makers need a common vision." The Twelve C's are an attempt to translate a common vision from words on a page or in a statement of goals into something that can be applied in the classroom.

REFERENCES

1. *Ontario Provincial Committee on Aims and Objectives of Education in the Schools of Ontario.* Toronto: Ontario Ministry of Education, 1968, pp. 14-15.

2. George Radwanski. *Ontario Study of the Relevance of Education and the Issue of Dropouts.* Toronto: Ontario Ministry of Education, 1987, p. 11.

3. Department of Education and Science. *The School Curriculum.* London: Her Majesty's Stationery Office, 1981.

4. *For the Love of Learning: Report of the Royal Commission on Learning.* Toronto: Queen's Printer, 1994, VOL. V, pp. 4-5.

5. H.G. Wells. *The Story of a Great Schoolmaster.* New York: Macmillan, 1924, p. 6.

Part 2

The Curriculum:
What Should Be
Taught and Learned?

CHAPTER THREE

What Is a Curriculum?

WHY DOES THE CURRICULUM MATTER?

A CURRICULUM CONVERTS THE general goals of education into more specific plans of action. It describes what teachers are expected to teach and therefore what students are required to learn. It organizes the sequence of courses from grade to grade and provides the basis for evaluation, whether of schools, students or teachers. It tells parents and the public at large what to expect of the schools. It is at the very centre of schooling.

Critics of schools have in recent years had much to say about the Canadian curriculum. Some of them see it as setting too low a standard for students. They point out that Canadian students are often two or three years behind students in Europe and Japan, especially in such subjects as mathematics and science. They complain that the curriculum does not give enough attention to such skills as problem-solving and critical thinking, so that students only memorize information but do not learn how to use it.

They also believe that most Canadian curricula contain too many elective courses after grade eight or nine and would like to see more in the way of a "core curriculum" of compulsory courses that all students must take. They believe that most curricula are too vague and general, so that teachers are not given enough direction about just what they are supposed to teach. Too often, they say, schools are allowed to treat curricula as guidelines they can follow

NB. concerns

or not, as they see fit, rather than as specific directives they must carry out. For the critics, the solution to all these problems is, first, to make the curriculum more demanding; second, to force teachers to stick to it; and third, to test students on it to see how well it has been taught and learned.

There is another kind of criticism directed, not at the standard, but at the content of the curriculum. Some critics see it as racist or sexist or not sensitive enough to cultural differences. For example, we see demands for curricula that are more multicultural, or designed specifically for First Nations or African-Canadian students, or for students of a particular religious group. We also see demands for more teaching of Holocaust studies, of black history, of ethnic history, of labour history, of comparative religion, of parenting skills, of more physical education and so on. On the other hand, some people object to what is already in the curriculum. They want to get rid of such books as *Huckleberry Finn* or *The Merchant of Venice*, or of topics they find offensive, such as evolution, sex education and certain political ideologies. Sometimes such demands take a more extreme form, as in the case of Christian fundamentalists' objections to the "secular humanism" that they believe pervades the entire curriculum.

In short, concern over the curriculum—its content, its purpose, its organization, its values, its standards—lies at the centre of much of the current discussion of education. This is not surprising, as the curriculum sets out what children are supposed to learn and so is, or ought to be, of great interest to parents and to the community in general.

It is puzzling why so few people have ever actually seen a school curriculum or spent any time discussing it. Curriculum documents are treated almost as state secrets, open only to the professionals. They are not to be found in bookstores or public libraries; unlike books and movies they are not reviewed in the newspapers; and they are certainly not available at the supermarket or the corner store. When we go to a new restaurant, we usually want to see a menu before we order. When we send our children to school, however, we rarely ask to see the curriculum it will be following. Therefore, it might be worth describing just what curricula are and how they came into existence.

DEVELOPMENT AND DESIGN OF A CURRICULUM

CURRICULA ARE DESIGNED BY MINISTRIES of education and issued under the authority of a minister of education, though ministers almost always follow the advice of their professional staff. There have been very few cases in Canada of political interference in curricula.

For the most part curricula are designed for a particular subject at a particular grade level and are supposed to be followed by all the schools in a province or territory. The only real exception to this pattern has been Ontario, which in the 1970s designed its provincial curricula as broad guidelines that set a general direction but allowed school boards to develop their own programs. In the 1990s, however, Ontario began to move toward the pattern of province-wide uniform curricula that other provinces had never abandoned. In all provinces, however, teachers had a good deal of freedom to adapt curricula to their particular circumstances, especially after inspectors and external examinations were discontinued in the late 1960s.

When ministries of education design curricula, they usually do so through committees of teachers that they select. These committees are chosen to represent different interests within the school system, for example, by region, by gender, or by type of school. They might be given a broad directive, for example, to develop a plan for a subject over a number of grade levels, say, high school mathematics or social studies from grades one to twelve; or a more specific task, say, to plan a Canadian history course for grade eleven or a science course for grade seven. Often, especially at the higher grade levels, university professors will also be asked to serve on curriculum committees.

From time to time, there have been attempts to open up the process of curriculum development by including non-professionals. In the 1970s the Manitoba Department of Education relaxed its monopoly of appointing people to curriculum committees. It asked the provincial teachers' society and the school trustees' and school superintendents' associations to nominate committee members, who acted, not as representatives of the department answerable to the minister of education, but as delegates of their organizations. The process was intended to give everyone in the school system a greater sense of ownership of new curricula, but was abandoned after some years when a new provincial government decided it wanted more direct control of the process. Depending on circumstances, curriculum committees will also ask for suggestions from a wide variety of groups, such as the women's movement, the First Nations, unions, chambers of commerce and professional organizations. In the past few years, as ministries of education shape education to meet economic priorities, the business community has been more involved in providing advice on what should be done.

In its simplest form, a curriculum is a course outline, say, for grade five health or grade ten geography, listing the topics to be taught and describing the details of the topics, usually with a short introductory statement of course goals and philosophy. Often these outlines are available separately, subject by subject, grade by grade, and sometimes they are combined for a grouping of grades, say, high school history or middle-years science. There may also be "support" and "resource" documents.

In the 1970s programs of study became more elaborate. They began to include statements of philosophy, descriptions of goals and objectives, explanations of teaching strategies, bibliographies and other pertinent materials. The positive result was that curriculum documents became a useful aid to teaching. The negative result was that they often became difficult to understand, partly because they contained so much material and partly because they were written in too technical a language. Even insiders sometimes found them confusing.

A few years ago, for example, I tried to find out what the provinces and territories were doing about the teaching of Canadian history. After consulting all the relevant curriculum documents from across the country, I found that, although I had more than thirty years' experience in the education system, I could not make sense of much of what I was reading. I wanted to answer two simple questions: in which grades was Canadian history taught and was it compulsory or elective? By the time I had finished, I did not know much more than when I had started. I understood why former British prime minister James Callaghan once called the curriculum a "secret garden," accessible only to those already in the know.

Even when we do understand a curriculum document, we must remember that it tells us only what a school is required to teach. It does not describe what actually happens in the classroom. Just because the curriculum sits on a shelf in the principal's office or in a teacher's cupboard, it does not follow that teachers actually use it. A few years back, the Manitoba Department of Education announced that it intended to test grade twelve social studies students and that the test would be based on the provincial curriculum. The department found itself swamped by requests for the curriculum from teachers who for years had been happily teaching as they pleased, all the time ignoring the curriculum they were supposed to be teaching.

This is not necessarily a bad thing, though it can certainly lead to abuses. In Alberta, James Keegstra was able to teach his anti-Semitic version of modern history for years because no one checked to see if he was following the provincial curriculum. On the other hand, dedicated and competent teachers, teaching something that they believed in and that was academically honest and accurate, might well do a better job than if they had to follow a curriculum they found professionally unacceptable.

Years ago, I was teaching a grade ten history class when I received an official visit from a provincial inspector. Having watched my lesson, he commented that I was not following the official curriculum. I told him that indeed I was not because the way it was set up did not make much sense to me. I was teaching the subject I was required to teach, in this case British history, but I was doing it my own way. To my relief, the inspector approved what I was doing. The fact remained, however, that the curriculum I was delivering was not the curriculum the province had planned or intended.

As well as this difference between what a curriculum says (sometimes called the curriculum-as-planned) and what a teacher actually does (curriculum-as-delivered), there may also be a difference between what teachers think they are doing and what students are actually learning, which we may think of as the curriculum-as-experienced. When teachers are asked which teaching methods they most often use, they frequently say "discussion." However, when students are asked a similar question, they reply "lecture." The explanation is probably that, when teachers use the word "discussion," they mean a combination of lecture with some questions and a bit of casual conversation, but students experience it as simply one more version of the sit-down-and-listen approach they expect from schools. Whatever the explanation, the classroom as experienced by students is often different from that experienced by teachers.

This is often referred to as the "hidden curriculum," meaning all those aspects of schooling not described in writing anywhere and that teachers are not aware of, but that nonetheless exert an important influence on what students learn. I came across a particularly vivid example of the hidden curriculum in action when I once asked a grade eight student what he was learning in a class I was visiting. I arrived at the classroom just as the teacher was settling the class down to work, and I wanted to find out what subject was in progress. The student, however, took my words literally and told me that the class was learning to copy down notes from the overhead projector, which was in fact all they did for the next forty minutes. The subject was supposed to be history, and the teacher no doubt believed himself to be working towards all kinds of worthy goals. The student, however, saw things for what they were. In fact, he was learning even more than he realized. Not only was he copying down notes, but he was doing so diligently and cheerfully, even though he saw no purpose in doing so. In short, he was learning to do an apparently pointless job in which he had no personal interest, and to do so willingly and without complaint. He was being effectively prepared for the adult working world. In the process he was also learning to dislike history as a subject and to narrow his options when, in later grades, he would have some chance to choose his courses.

Perhaps the greatest weakness of curriculum development in Canada has been the general failure to ensure that once curricula were developed, they actually got taught in the schools. The assumption was that once a curriculum had been developed and distributed, teachers would automatically teach it. A few in-service sessions were organized to introduce teachers and sometimes parents to a new curriculum, but then for the most part teachers were left on their own. Companies spend huge sums of money in marketing a new product; ministries of education simply assume that their new curriculum products will sell themselves. The predictable result has been that teachers often ignored new programs, which they often saw as likely to make their lives more difficult, which they had had no voice in developing and which they often regarded as unnecessary in the first place. As noted in Chapter 2, teachers usually think in terms of what is best for their students, not in terms of what the curriculum says; so once provincial examinations were discontinued in the late 1960s, they were free to do as they pleased.

Universities and employers grumbled that they no longer knew what a grade twelve diploma meant, that even when students had the same course credits, they had not necessarily studied the same things. Educators largely dismissed such complaints and insisted that they must be free to adapt curricula to their students. What critics saw as inefficient chaos, teachers saw as healthy flexibility. In the 1990s, however, things began to change. Canadians began to wonder if their schools were as good as they should be. Some Canadians experienced a minor panic when international tests suggested that Canadian students had fallen behind students in other countries. Education ministries became more receptive to the complaints of the business world. Schools were expected to make their contribution to Canada's global competitiveness. As a result, we now see a growing demand both to upgrade the quality of the curriculum and to make sure that teachers follow it more closely.

OUTCOMES AND OBJECTIVES

FOR THE MOST PART, people have thought of the curriculum in terms of subjects to be taught. The curriculum is, in effect, a set of instructions to schools, telling them what to teach. Many curriculum planners, however, see this as putting the cart before the horse. They point out that just because teachers teach something does not mean students learn it. After a few years in school most students have mastered the art of looking attentive while their minds are elsewhere.

This is why the planners say we should think of curricula in terms of what students are supposed to *learn*, rather than what teachers are supposed to teach. And since there must be ways to find out what students have learned, we have to think of student learning in ways that can be measured, such as tests, essay writing, mathematical problem-solving, finding information on the Internet and fixing engines in autoshops. The whole point of education, in this view, is that students learn something that they otherwise did not know or could not do. In the words of the 1993 New Brunswick Commission on Excellence in Education:

> Students, teachers, parents, trustees, and the Department all have legitimate reasons to know what is being attempted and when it has been achieved. It is not unreasonable to ask what a child should know and be able to do by the end of grade 6. What level of proficiency in reading, writing, and numbers is it reasonable to assume has been mastered? What kinds of literature have been read and understood? What kinds of exercises in

the gathering and organizing of information can be
conducted? What evidence of scientific reasoning
can be expected?[1]

The idea is that when parents, employers, universities and colleges, and teachers and students, for that matter, have a clear idea of
what is being done in schools, and why, and also have some evidence
that what is happening is what is supposed to happen, then schooling will be more effective. In a sense the language of objectives and
outcomes is intended to serve a kind of truth-in-advertising purpose
in education.

This approach to curriculum thinks not in terms of teacher
"inputs" but of student "outcomes." To take a specific example, a
teacher should not say, "I will teach the War of 1812," but rather,
"After studying the War of 1812 students will be able to identify certain names, dates and events, to write a short essay, to present an
argument in a debate, and to summarize a passage from a book."
Here are a few of the reading outcomes set out for Ontario grade
three students:

- understand a story and predict what may happen next;
- learn new words through reading;
- interpret simple diagrams, charts and maps;
- follow written directions;
- understand the purpose of spelling and punctuation
  and use them correctly to make meaning clear.[2]

This approach to designing the curriculum as a series of outcomes seems to be catching on with ministries of education across
Canada. They see it as a way to make schools more accountable for
their performance and as a way of making it clearer to parents what
schools do. In 1993 the New Brunswick Department of Education
reported that it intended to design its entire curriculum in terms of
outcomes. Using the language of industry, it said that all existing
curricula would be rewritten to "define 'up-front' the end
products to be achieved in education" and all new curricula would
"clearly specify intended learning outcomes."[3] The Ontario Royal
Com-mission on Learning in 1994 similarly recommended that
"learner outcomes" be clearly specified in core curricula. The western
Canadian provinces began in the 1990s to look for ways to make

their curricula more similar, first in mathematics and science, then in language arts and social studies. To do so, they have not specified that particular subjects should be taught the same way at all grade levels in every province. Instead, they have defined the "outcomes" they want students to achieve, leaving it to each province to decide just what content should be used to achieve them. Across the country, the outcomes army is on the march.

Outcomes describe what students must be able to do as a result of studying a particular topic. When outcomes are thought of as things for teachers or students to aim at, they are described as "objectives." So the teacher's task becomes not to think in terms of "I will teach the war of 1812," but to ensure that students can identify important dates, names and events, and can complete whatever tasks are specified. In addition, students themselves should be made aware of these objectives, for then they will know exactly what they are supposed to do and so will study more effectively. Outside the school, parents and others, once they know the objectives, will be able to tell whether or not the school is doing its job.

Some supporters of this approach believe that teaching should be organized in terms of "behavioural objectives," by which they mean we can know whether an objective has been achieved only by noticing a change in a student's behaviour. This does not mean that schools are supposed to turn students into different kinds of people through some sort of brainwashing, but rather that students must be able to do something we can see before we can say they have in fact learned something. If we say we have given students a love of reading, we have to be able to point to something specific to prove it. Perhaps they read more books, or go to the library more often, or talk about books. At the extreme, believers in behavioural objectives claim that teachers must be able to specify exactly what students should be able to do and under what conditions. For example, a complete behavioural objective would read something like this: "Students will list the main battles of the War of 1812 in the correct chronological order, from memory, in three minutes or less."

This kind of objective has attracted a fair amount of criticism. Teachers object that they simply do not have the time to convert everything they teach into this amount of detail. They also argue that, as trained professionals, they know what they are doing, so that it would be a waste of time and effort to spell everything out like this.

A more philosophical objection to behavioural objectives is that they limit teaching to the achievement of pre-set and measurable objectives and ignore the very things that should be at the centre of education, in particular, to help students do the unexpected. Measurable behavioural objectives might be useful when it comes to testing the learning of specific facts and skills, but not for more powerful forms of thinking. In the words of the literary critic, Northrop Frye: "The difference between a good and a mediocre teacher lies mainly in the emphasis the former puts on the exploring part of the mind, the aspects of learning that reveal meanings and lead to further understanding."[4] And the exploring part of the mind is, by definition, unpredictable. It cannot be described in terms of pre-set objectives. All teachers have experienced the thrill of finding students beginning to think for themselves in unpredictable ways.

I remember teaching a grade twelve class about the French Revolution when one student, who was not one of the academic stars of the class, burst out, "No matter what happens, it seems it's the poor who always lose." It was not perhaps an earthshaking discovery, but it was an original idea for him and showed me he was thinking seriously about what I was teaching. His comment also provided the basis for further discussion: What should poor people do? When are revolutions justified? Are the potential gains worth the risk? Is history nothing but the story of the powerful? This kind of learning cannot be accounted for in terms of behavioural objectives. In fact, if the achievement of such objectives becomes the test of effective teaching, teachers will find themselves in a straitjacket, which will prevent them from shaping their teaching to their students. And in the not-so-long run, the free spirits we want to attract to teaching will see no future in it.

The outcomes or objectives approach to curriculum development takes no subject for granted. It does not say, for example, "We must teach history." Rather, it says, "Students must gain a sound understanding of the causes of war," and goes on to ask: "What is the best way to do this?" Any given subject must answer a tough question: Is it the most effective way to achieve the specified objectives? If it is, well and good. If it is not, then it must make way for something else. If, for example, the objective is to make students literate and literacy is defined as reading and writing at certain measurable levels, then whether using great literature or science fiction or technical manuals or even comic books is the best way to do it remains an open question.

This whole question of objectives and outcomes is not some abstract theoretical discussion, of concern only to professional educators. It raises fundamental questions about what we want from schools and how we want them to do it. At its best, it helps us to think of schooling in terms of what we want students to learn, shakes us loose from taken-for-granted assumptions, and offers a way to achieve greater public involvement in education. At its worst, it threatens to turn teaching into a mechanical process of training students to pass tests, while unnecessarily restricting teachers' freedom to open their students' minds. Here, as elsewhere in education, we must be careful not to jump on bandwagons. Objectives are well and good in their place and we should use them to the extent that they are useful, which is mostly in the learning of specific facts and skills. At the same time, we should not let them become the be-all and end-all of education. Teaching is full of opportunities to lead students along unexpected paths. Once students are involved in a topic, regardless of their so-called ability, they are likely to ask all sorts of unanticipated questions. It would be a tragedy if, by concentrating too tightly on pre-specified objectives and outcomes, we prevented students and teachers from pursuing those questions.

SUBJECTS OR LEARNING EXPERIENCES?

As the popularity of the outcomes/objectives approach shows, these days no subject can take its place in the curriculum for granted. Some educators, in fact, favour getting rid of subjects altogether. They argue that we do not think in terms of subjects in our daily lives. Rather, we face problems or have experiences and draw on all aspects of our knowledge to deal with them. And if this is true of adults, it is even truer of children. Subjects, this argument goes, are adult inventions for classifying knowledge. They might make sense for research and university purposes; they do not make sense for children. Indeed, very often children do not have the maturity, the experience or the mental capacity to understand them. No one expects a young child, for example, to understand algebra or chemistry.

Therefore, the argument continues, instead of teaching subjects in the schools, we should organize the curriculum around themes or topics that will interest students while also teaching them the necessary knowledge and skills. To some extent teachers already do this with younger children, as in the case of all those projects on dinosaurs, space travel, rain forests, pollution, and the rest, which involve art, literature, music, science, history and geography, as well as a range of other subjects. Some teachers pursue it with older students also. Many school systems operate what are usually described as "alternative" schools or programs for students who reject the conventional curriculum. Such schools look for activities or projects that will interest students while at the same time providing the academic learning they need. They do not begin with subjects such as science and history but with what they think their students need to learn and then draw on the subjects as needed.

Some years ago, Peter McLaren described his attempts to teach a class of grade six students in inner-city Toronto. Though he established good personal relations with his students, they continually resisted his efforts to teach them subjects that were light-years removed from their own interests and concerns in a conventional manner. As McLaren described his experience:

> I finally accepted the fact that my students needed to be taught on their own terms. The traditional middle-class images of success were not open to them, images which, they, in turn, were able to resist. In the classroom, they had become, understandably, street-wise cynical about the social candy of academic rewards such as good grades on term papers or tests. I began to be successful with these students when I accepted their social outlook as the starting point. [5]

Looking back on his experience, he later concluded it would have made more sense to organize his program, not around the usual school subjects of social studies, language arts, science and the rest, but instead around the experiences and problems his students and their families faced, the most pressing of which was poverty. Such a program would have seemed relevant to the students, established links with parents and the community, connected learning with the real world, while also teaching the expected academic skills.

Some educators believe that all students would benefit if the various subjects of the curriculum were more integrated than they are. Some see an "integrated curriculum" as being especially useful with students in the middle school range, roughly between grades five and eight, though it has been used at all grade levels. In its most moderate version, it takes the form of bringing two or more subjects together whenever they can reinforce each other. For example, if students were studying ancient Greece in history, they might also study Greek mythology in their literature course, and work with ancient Greek themes in art. They could also pursue some aspects of the topic in mathematics and science, since the Greeks made important contributions to geometry and had well-developed views of science. In a stronger version than this, the integrated approach chooses themes or topics, for example, war, the environment, or the community, and organizes the whole curriculum around them. Both approaches are becoming easier to put in place as schools across the country begin to establish interdisciplinary teaching teams in which three or four teachers from different subject backgrounds share responsibility for a group of about ninety or so children and have some degree of control over their own timetable, so that the integration of the curriculum is more easily done.

The idea of curriculum integration is not some new-fangled fad. It has a long history, going back at least to the 1890s. In the 1920s the American educationist, W.H. Kilpatrick, called it the "project" method, and it became popular with some Canadian teachers between the two world wars. A Canadian version of it was pioneered in Alberta by the educationist Donalda Dickie of Calgary, who called it the "enterprise" method. Both Kilpatrick and Dickie urged teachers to organize their curricula, not on the basis of subjects, but around topics or problems that were both appealing to students and taken from the world in which they lived. Back in the 1920s an American curriculum expert put it this way:

> The starting point of curriculum organization will not be the learning of the facts in subjects called "geography," economics," and "civics;" it will be, rather, a realistic problem of individual and social life with which young people will grapple directly. One question and one only should guide our search for a sound curriculum organization: What meanings and attitudes must be developed as integrated

> units to enable juvenile minds (or adult minds for
> that matter!) to understand modes of living and
> social problems?[6]

Defenders of the subjects were horrified. They saw this new approach as leading to a lowering of standards, a dumbing-down of learning, a refusal to challenge students and an abandonment of the heritage of human civilization. In their view, integrating the subjects into themes or projects would result in important knowledge being ignored, since only the things that were thought to be interesting to students and able to be integrated with something else would be taught. History for example, would not be taught as a subject in its own right, as a systematic study of the past. Instead, teachers would choose the bits of it that could be integrated into a theme or that illustrated something in the news and forget the rest. As a result, large chunks of history, and of all other subjects, would simply be ignored.

As happens so often in education, the argument quickly became what it still largely remains—an exchange of slogans and stereotypes, with little connection to the real world of education. In schools as they actually exist, subjects are sometimes taught badly, with the result that students receive none of the benefits claimed for them. This was why curriculum reformers abandoned subject-based teaching for themes and projects and integrated approaches in the first place. At the same time, however, integrated teaching is not necessarily better just because it is integrated. To do it well requires time, resources and training that many teachers do not have. One of the strongest arguments against integrating the curriculum is that it demands more from teachers by way of knowledge, planning and working together than they can usually deliver, especially given the working conditions they typically face.

Moreover, integrating the curriculum does not at all answer the question of what exactly we should be teaching students. It deals only with the question of how to organize a curriculum, not what should go into it in the first place. Before we can say whether it makes sense to integrate a curriculum, we must first decide what the curriculum should contain. When done well, both subject-based teaching and integrated teaching can benefit students. The secret of success lies not in the automatic adoption of one or the other, but in doing either or both properly.

REFERENCES

1. New Brunswick Commission on Excellence in Education. *Schools for a New Century.* Fredericton, New Brunswick Department of Education, 1993, p. 15.

2. *The Common Curriculum.* Toronto: Ontario Ministry of Education, 1993.

3. New Brunswick Department of Education. *Education 2000: Preparing Students for the New Century.* Fredericton, 1993, p. 27.

4. Northrop Frye (ed.). *Design for Learning.* Toronto: University of Toronto Press, 1962, p. 12.

5. Peter McLaren. *Cries from the Corridor.* Markham: Paperjacks, 1981, p. 209.

6. Harold Rugg. *American Life and the School Curriculum: Next Steps Toward Schools of Living.* Boston: Ginn, 1936, p. 333.

CHAPTER FOUR

What Should Students Learn?

KNOWLEDGE, SKILLS AND VALUES

WHATEVER OUR PARTICULAR PHILOSOPHY of education, most of us
expect the schools to teach our children three types of things:
knowledge, skills and values. We expect our children to learn all
kinds of facts and information they would not learn anywhere else.
We want them, however, to be more than walking encyclopaedias,
and so we expect them to learn a whole range of skills—academic,
musical, artistic, social, physical and technical. And we also expect
the schools to teach values, or at least to reinforce the values that we
teach at home. We want children to behave properly, to get along
with other people, to tell the truth and so on. Obviously we often
disagree about just what all this involves and how it is best done. We
do not always share the same values, or value the same knowledge
and skills. Whatever our beliefs might be, however, most of us expect
the schools to teach some kind of knowledge, skills and values. And
these days most curricula are organized in terms of all three.

THE IMPORTANCE OF KNOWLEDGE

KNOWLEDGE, IN THE SENSE of basic factual information, is an
important element of the curriculum. At least, it ought to be—
but schools in recent years have not valued it as they should. Very
few curriculum documents, in any subject, make it clear just what

students are supposed to know. Skills and self-esteem often get more emphasis than knowledge. Here are the goals of one junior high school as formulated in the 1980s:

- to improve basic academic skills;
- to improve self-understanding;
- to improve self-worth and self respect;
- to acquire a greater sense of self-direction;
- to increase a sense of self-awareness;
- to acquire skills for more effective living.

These are important goals, but what is notable about this list, besides its heavy emphasis on self, is its failure to say anything about what students should *know*. Obviously students will learn something as they strive to meet the goals described on the list, but nothing is said about what this something is.

Schools have moved in this direction for good reasons. It is, in part, a reaction against the drudgery of much fact-based teaching in the past, where students memorized things they never really understood or cared about, took a test and then promptly forgot them. It is also a response to the problems schools face, for the reality is that many students do not feel good about themselves, do not have much faith in the future, do not have a sense of direction, and so are not very interested in learning what schools want to teach. Since no one else seems to be doing much about it, schools have moved in to fill the gap. And schools are too easily persuaded by the false argument that factual information is not all that important, that what matters is knowing how to find information when you need it.

This is not just the argument of trendy educationists. Here is a senior executive of the Motorola corporation in 1996:

> Memorized facts, which are the basis for most testing done in schools today, are of little use in the age in which information is doubling every two or three years. We have expert systems in computing and the Internet that can provide the facts we need when we need them. Our workforce needs to utilize the facts to assist in developing solutions to problems. The worker needs to be able to utilize the systems that give him or her

access to information when it's required in the
problem-solving process.[1]

One can see why an industry would like to get workers with lots
of skills but who know nothing apart from the skills. Without
knowledge, they will have no basis for questioning anything. And
with skills they will know how to do what they are told. But even if
as workers we can somehow manage without knowledge, we certainly cannot as citizens and as human beings.

One reason we send children to school is to learn facts—and
plenty of them. We expect them to learn, for instance, some basic
history and geography, and arts and science. We expect them to
learn things their parents do not know, say, in algebra, a second language, or physics. Schools expand students' horizons by introducing
them to aspects of life they might otherwise never encounter. In my
own case, it was in school that I first listened to classical music,
looked at great art, learned French and Latin, learned to play tennis
and rugby football, and so on and so on—none of which I would
have learned anywhere else. I did not necessarily like it all, but I
experienced things that gave me a greater range of choices than I
otherwise would have had and than my parents had ever had.
Thanks to my teachers, I knew more or less how electricity worked,
and understood the principles behind the radio and the telephone.
Little of this knowledge has been directly useful to me in any practical sense. If I need electrical work done, I call an electrician. But at
least I understand what is going on in the world around me and as a
result feel that much more in control of my life. To be without
knowledge is like living in a country where you do not know a word
of the language and so can never figure out what is going on.

All this may sound obvious, but there is an educational theory
that argues that we do not need to carry a lot of information in our
heads. It runs as follows: one, there is more knowledge in the world
than we can ever know and it is increasing all the time; two, we can
never tell in advance what knowledge we might need; three, knowledge often becomes out-of-date thanks to new inventions and discoveries; and four, knowledge is easily available, in everything from
reference books to CD-ROMS. Therefore, what we really need is to
learn how to find and use information when we require it.

This is only superficially true. Without a great deal of everyday
knowledge in our heads, we could barely survive. A person who has

lost his or her memory, and is therefore without any knowledge, is helpless. And once one moves beyond bare survival, the problem becomes even more acute. Without knowledge, we can never make sense of the world around us. Here is a list of terms and phrases taken out of the local newspaper on the day I write these words: *NHL Western Conference, El Niño, Stanley Cup, International Olympic Committee, Nigerian military junta, Liberal backbencher, Tory backroom player, a UN division of Palestine, the equatorial Pacific, the Holocaust, Columbia Icefield, the House of Commons, cabinet minister, Crown corporation, Meech Lake accord, RCMP, developing countries, Shamattawa First Nation, small-c conservative.* Our lives are full of terms like these, whether the subject is politics, sport, hobbies, work, or anything else. To understand them, and thus to understand what is going on around us, so that we are not overwhelmed by it, we need not only the "information processing skills" so beloved of today's school reformers, but factual knowledge, not waiting to be accessed in a computer but already stored in our heads.

Moreover, such knowledge helps make a society what it is. Many of the terms just listed are uniquely Canadian and make sense only to Canadians or people who know something about Canada. They are knowledge that Canadians share as Canadians, reminding us that we share a common country, with a common history and common problems. In teaching this kind of knowledge, schools help children gain a sense of national identity. This is an especially important task in Canada, where so much of the information our children pick up deals not with Canada but with the United States, with the result that they often know more about American than Canadian life.

This kind of knowledge has been described as "cultural literacy" by the American writer E.D. Hirsch in his book of that name. He argues that the existence of any society depends on its people sharing a common body of knowledge that helps them understand one another and gives them some sense of common identity. If one person says to another, "Well, I'm no Wayne Gretzky" or "Who do you think you are—Einstein?" they both need to understand the point of the references. And every society has thousands of such references in its everyday life. Hirsch sees the ability to understand them as the basis of the shared experience that makes a society possible. He also sees this shared knowledge as providing the basis for educational success, since people who possess it will be better able to make sense of everything they see and hear taking place around them.

Hirsch's idea of cultural literacy has considerable relevance for Canada, where a very real need exists for Canadian school curricula to teach Canadian students more about the country in which they live. To take only one example, not long ago I sat in a class of bright and enthusiastic grade eleven students who were busily arguing about whether Canada is a monarchy—not whether it should or should not be, but whether it is. The students did not realize there was no cause for argument. Whether we like it or not, Canada is, as a matter of fact, a monarchy. Here, as in so much else, students misunderstood their own country. In these circumstances, a Canadian version of Hirsch's cultural literacy would provide a useful service.

WHAT SHOULD STUDENTS KNOW?

MOST OFTEN, RECOMMENDATIONS ABOUT what students should know have come in the form of lists of subjects, which are seen as making up a "core curriculum" all students must take. In 1988 the Royal Commission on Education in British Columbia recommended a common curriculum for all students from grades one to ten, consisting of four groupings of subjects: humanities (mainly literature, languages and social studies); fine arts; sciences; and practical arts (physical education, health, guidance and life skills); followed in grades eleven and twelve by compulsory physical education, two years of English, two years of history and a one-year course in science, technology and the environment, with a range of elective courses geared towards further education and careers.

In 1993 a New Brunswick commission recommended that all students from grades one to eight must take a common curriculum in four areas: languages and social studies; mathematics and science; fine arts; and practical arts (physical education, technology and vocational skills). From grades nine to twelve, the commission recommended that the number of compulsory courses should be increased, that all elective courses be geared towards jobs and job skills, and that all students must take four courses in mathematics and three in science.

The 1994 Royal Commission in Ontario said much the same thing, recommending that all students take the same curriculum to the end of grade nine and that it be organized into four groupings of subjects: language; mathematics, science and technology; the arts; and "self and society," which was defined as social studies, business education, family studies, guidance, health and physical education. It also recommended a reduction in elective courses from grades ten to twelve, with the compulsory courses to include three credits in English or French, a second language for all students, two social science credits, two credits each in science and mathematics, as well as credits in the arts, life skills, physical education and technology.

These recommendations—and there are many others like them across Canada—are based on five assumptions. One, schools have a responsibility to introduce students to the full range of human knowledge. Two, this can best be done through the conventional subjects, such as English, history, science, mathematics, art and music. Three, a basic knowledge of these subjects is an important part of what it means to be educated. Four, this basic knowledge forms a foundation on which students can make choices concerning further education and careers as they get older. Five, it provides a basis upon which students will grow up to become successful workers, able to find and hold a job; good citizens, able to participate in and contribute to society; and well-rounded human beings, able to make the most of their lives.

These recommendations also illustrate a trend that can be seen in all parts of Canada. Ministries of education are now requiring schools to teach more compulsory courses and to follow centrally designed curricula. By and large, the new compulsory curricula follow a common pattern, driven by what curriculum planners believe to be the needs of the economy. Most attention is given to language and mathematics, or to "literacy " and "numeracy," to use the language of education. Science and technology, including computer studies, come a close second, with history, social studies, literature and the arts following a considerable distance behind.

Teachers have reacted to these developments in various ways. Some have received them with open arms, seeing the chance to win greater resources in school-business partnerships, and welcoming what they see as a move that will make schooling more relevant to students. Others reject them, condemning the downgrading of history, literature and the arts as an abandonment of the schools' traditional concern with citizenship and all-round development, and likely to reduce education to job training.

The majority of teachers, however, concentrate more on what the new trends in curriculum will mean for students. They worry that cutting back elective courses and insisting that all students must

follow a common curriculum will lead to higher failure and dropout
rates. They believe that teaching will become more difficult, since
teachers will have less freedom to adapt the curriculum to the needs
of their students.

Telling schools what to teach can create problems. How does
one decide just what it is all students must know? Public opinion
surveys will not provide the answer. The experts disagree with each
other. Even when we can agree that some subject must be taught, we
often disagree on just what parts of it should be included in the curriculum or how it should be presented. We can all agree, for example, that students should learn to read. But what should they read
once they are literate? And just what is literacy? I was once part of a
delegation petitioning a minister of education to reverse his decision
to scrap a year of Canadian history when he told us that he wanted
to emphasize literacy. Absolutely, we replied, and what better way to
teach literacy than through reading history? He told us that was not
what he meant at all. He favoured "pure literacy." I still have not
figured out what that is.

Should students read Shakespeare or comic books? I would
choose Shakespeare every time. His use of language is so much
richer than any alternative. But what do we do with students who for
whatever reason find Shakespeare a barrier to reading rather than an
incentive? We can agree that Canadian history should be taught, but
since there is only so much time in the school year, how should we
balance the time given to the British conquest of Quebec against the
First and Second World Wars, the Selkirk Settlement against the
Winnipeg General Strike, the Atlantic fishery against the Western
fur trade, especially when historians themselves do not have answers
to such questions? The United States spent millions of dollars in the
1990s drawing up a set of national standards for history, only to find
them roundly attacked for their alleged omissions and biases.

Even if we can agree about what should be taught, there is
always the risk that teachers will not be able to teach it successfully.
If the curriculum is too restrictive, too filled with content, too controlled by examinations or too far removed from the concerns of
students, teachers will not have the freedom they need to adapt it to
their students. I taught high school history when there were all-or-
nothing provincial examinations that counted for one hundred per
cent of a student's mark, thus ensuring that teachers stuck to the
provincial curriculum. I continued to teach it after examinations

were abolished, and I am convinced that I was a better teacher without external examinations than with them. Once they had gone, I was free to adjust what I was teaching to the nature of my students. I could speed up or slow down as needed. I could stop and pursue a topic if it caught students' interest or skim over it if it was not going anywhere. I did not cover the same amount of content I once had, but what I did cover I taught in far more depth, with the result that my students learned what history was really all about as a subject and as a way of thinking. Instead of racing through the First World War in a week, I could spend a month or more on it if it made educational sense. It meant that other topics had to be sacrificed or received only slight attention, but what the students learned, they learned with a depth and a richness that would otherwise have been impossible to achieve. History became no longer one-damn-thing-after-another but an in-depth exploration of the human experience, or at least as in-depth as it is possible to be at a grade twelve level. Students in grade twelve, however, are at a particularly powerful age to raise questions of human motivation and behaviour. And, as with history, so with most other subjects.

Teachers sometimes speak of the "teaching moment," when students come to life and it becomes possible to take them in directions one would not have thought possible. No curriculum should be so tightly controlled that it prevents teachers from adapting it to the students they teach. The problem is that there is no way of deciding in advance and in the abstract where to draw the line between compulsion and freedom. This is a decision that can be made only in light of the specific circumstances of a teacher working with a particular class. Here, as so often happens, we face the central fact of schooling: everything depends on the professional skill of the teacher. With good teachers, a compulsory curriculum is irrelevant. With bad teachers, no amount of compulsion will do the trick.

As good teachers recognize, however, learning is not just a matter of knowing how to look things up, whether in the library or on the computer. It is easy to dismiss factual knowledge as mere memory work, but this knowledge matters. Some sociologists maintain that school knowledge is nothing more than official ideology, but even if this were true, we still need to give students access to it, if only for their own protection. In fact, however, knowledge is more than this. It gives us access to what the nineteenth-century writer, Matthew Arnold, described as the best that has been thought and written. It helps us gain control of our lives while also making them more interesting and useful.

THE PLACE OF SKILLS

As IMPORTANT AS FACTUAL knowledge is, it obviously is not enough. We can never learn everything in school that we will need to know in later life, and what we do learn can become outdated as a result of new discoveries and theories. Facts on their own can take us only so far. We must be able to use them in some way. We have to be able to find, learn and sort out information. We have to be able to take in what is useful and reject what is not. We have to be able to separate the true or the probable from the false. We have to be able to think. Since much of our information comes from face-to-face conversation, we also have to know how to express our ideas, how to argue for them, especially when other people's opinions are different from ours. And life is not just a matter of the mind; it requires us to use our bodies, to interact with other people, to look after ourselves and others, to hold down a job. In a word we need skills.

Education has always been concerned with skills. No doubt some of the very first teaching was how to make a flint axe, how to hunt, and how to read tracks. In ancient Greece and Rome, the skill of public speaking, which also involved the skills of finding information, organizing it and thinking about it, was especially valued. In the Middle Ages, skill in argument and debate was a key goal of education.

Today schools tend to dismiss memory work, but memorizing in and of itself is a skill. In the Middle Ages teachers spent much time and effort training their students to improve their memories. By the end of the nineteenth century, as governments began to establish public school systems, certain skills came to be seen as basic. They began with the famous three R's—of reading, writing and arithmetic—and included what were seen as useful work and citizenship skills.

Until the early 1970s, however, we concentrated largely on teaching facts and for the most part ignored skills. Canadian schools were dominated by provincial examinations, which tested little beyond the repetition of facts. When I marked provincial history examinations in Manitoba in the 1960s, I found that I had to follow a carefully organized marking plan in which almost all the marks were awarded for facts, with nothing left over for argument or point of view. I was told that the reason for this state of affairs was that this was all that could be marked fairly and objectively on a province-wide basis.

When I began teaching history, I collected examination papers from previous years and made a chart showing what questions were set in which years. These questions showed that any history course in fact revolved around ten or so topics. The task of teaching history, therefore, became making sure that students had a reasonable grasp of these topics and a bag of tricks for answering examination questions. It was not especially difficult to do, provided that students were willing to work, and it could be done in ways that students found friendly enough; but I thought then, as I think now, that it was only a shadow of what education ought to be.

I welcomed the end of provincial examinations. I felt set free. Now I could really teach students to think and argue. I could get them beyond the facts to consider such questions as: Was Peter the Great really great? Who or what defeated Napoleon? In other words, I could spend more time than ever before teaching not just facts, but skills.

Through the 1960s and into the 1970s, educators produced ever more detailed lists of skills, though the ideas behind them were straightforward enough. The essential skills were those of research (reading, and finding and using information); communication (speaking, listening, writing and arguing); critical thinking and analysis; problem-solving; planning and organizing work; and working with other people. Subjects such as physical education, home economics and industrial arts went further and included a variety of physical and occupational and other skills. None of this was totally new. Teachers had always known that skills were important and had never completely neglected them, but the abolition of fact-based examinations and the move to tie education more closely to the economy created something of a skills mania.

The danger of this new enthusiasm for skills was that, in reacting against the old-style teaching of facts-for-the-sake-of-facts, we sometimes threw the baby out with the bathwater. After all, if critical thinking is the goal, what does it matter what students use to learn to think more critically? They can use a cartoon, an advertisement, an editorial or a letter to the editor just as easily as something from history or science or any other subject. Some skill enthusiasts insisted that subject matter was unimportant anyway, that skills could be separated from content and taught as courses in their own right.

By the 1990s some educators began to talk of "generic" skills, meaning skills that can be used anywhere, in any context, and do not depend on the possession of specific knowledge. In the words of a 1990 Ontario report:

> With the advent of new information-based tech-
> nology and the shift to a more flexible and multi-
> skilled workforce, employers are finding that
> generic workplace skills are becoming increasingly
> important relative to job-specific skills. Generic
> skills are those which workers can use in many
> jobs. They include analytical, problem-solving,
> workplace interpersonal and broad technical skills
> that may be found in the skilled trades or in the
> operation of personal computers.[2]

Across the country, schools are now urged to concentrate on the skills needed in the workplace. They have responded by introducing courses in life skills, skills for independent living, entrepreneurship and the like. If the new global economy requires a flexible, adaptable workforce, skilled at decision-making, problem-solving and social interaction, then the curriculum will be organized accordingly. In the process, certain questions are not being asked. The new work-place skills will not give workers more power in the workplace, but only make them more productive in doing what they are assigned to do. Workers' new skills of decision-making, critical thinking and problem-solving are not intended to raise the question of who is in charge and why, but only to get the job done more quickly. And there is no guarantee that the new skilled jobs will exist in any great numbers. Many of the jobs that are available are "McJobs"—part-time, low wage and requiring few of the new sophisticated skills. In other words, despite the promises of the skills enthusiasts, it is far from certain that the skills currently being singled out will match the workplace of the future for most workers.

Nonetheless, skills are important and no curriculum should ignore them. Literacy, critical thinking, problem-solving, decision-making, analysis, research, communication and interacting with other people are important, not so much for work as for citizen-ship and for life generally. Schools must teach them, not as abstract, so-called generic exercises, but in the context of rich and valuable subject matter. Properly taught, facts and skills are not opposed to each other; they are two sides of the same coin. They must be a fundamental part of every subject in the curriculum, demonstrated in everything a teacher does, emphasized in tests and examinations, and reinforced by the work of the school as a whole.

MORALS AND VALUES

BESIDES KNOWLEDGE AND SKILLS, most curriculum documents say something about values. The 1988 British Columbia Royal Commission described "moral and civic development" as one of the four goals of schooling. The 1994 Ontario Royal Commission was more specific, speaking of the responsibility of schools to teach "some sense of honesty, truth, civility, social justice, and co-operation, and a determination to combat violence, racism, gender inequality, and environmental degradation." As the Royal Commission went on to note, there will be people who find some of these values controversial and perhaps even unacceptable in some cases, but such is the nature of values.[3]

In most cases, the values that are emphasized in schools include respect for others, tolerance, regard for human rights, a sense of responsibility, honesty, and a work ethic. Schools begin teaching these values from the very first day students enter their doors. Young children are taught to share, to work and play together, to follow instructions, to act responsibly, both through example and through direct instruction. As they get older, this kind of teaching becomes less necessary, though it can never be totally put aside. Even senior students sometimes have to be reminded how to behave or how to treat other people. And whether teachers teach them directly or not, values are transmitted by the very structure and organization of a school. For example, schools do not tolerate violence, abusive behaviour, bad language, disrespect for others or other forms of antisocial behaviour. At a well-run school values are taught as part of its daily routines. Even well-swept hallways and a general air of order and cleanliness have a lesson to teach, which is why, for example, schools take such care to erase graffiti whenever they occur.

Values can become controversial, however, when schools begin to tackle issues of right and wrong, as they inevitably must. It is next to impossible to teach some subjects without raising questions concerning values and morality. A teacher would have to be unconscious not to touch on the values in such novels as Margaret Lawrence's *The Diviners*, William Golding's *Lord of the Flies* or George Orwell's *Nineteen Eighty-Four*, to take only three of the many books that some people have tried to ban from schools from time to time. And even if teachers tried to avoid the values in such books, their students would inevitably raise them. There is little that a teenager likes more than a good argument about some issue of fairness or morality.

Social studies are also full of values. Many social studies courses are deliberately organized around controversial social and political problems, usually called "public issues," ranging from abortion to drugs, from gun control to strikes, on which parents often have very strong opinions. Even history, despite dealing with the dead and gone, cannot avoid controversy, as I found out years ago when I was gently told off by various parents for raising questions about religious leaders of the Protestant Reformation of the sixteenth century. Even after four hundred years, history still had the power to shock. Fortunately for me, my parent critics were amused rather than annoyed but, as history teachers continually discover, history is far from dead. Even science cannot avoid values, as any science teacher learns when a creationist parent raises objections to the teaching of evolution. And science teachers who consider the social implications of science, as many do, cannot avoid the values in such topics as environmental protection, genetic engineering, cloning, and the use of animals in experiments. As for family life and sex education, the objections can come thick and fast.

There are some Christian fundamentalists who insist that all subjects must be taught without raising any opinions or issues at all. History, literature, science and the rest must be taught only as fact, and anything that is not fact must be banned from the classroom. It might work for algebra or irregular French verbs, but not for much else. No teacher I have ever known, not even the most dedicated fact merchants, could teach this way. And even if it could be done, it makes for very dull teaching and a very narrow view of learning.

If schools are to educate, they have to open students' minds to ideas and experiences they have never thought of before, even at the risk of controversy. Anything less will prevent the schools preparing students for citizenship in the Canadian democracy. The 1988 British Columbia Royal Commission on Education put it this way:

> Young people at school today are forced to con-
> sider many difficult moral issues and their consid-
> eration of such issues is made even more
> problematic by the diversity in social values that
> marks the society in which they live. They must
> learn to answer for themselves, for the future
> generation they represent, an array of ethical
> questions . . . in the realms of social relations,
> science, technology, and medicine. Through educa-
> tion, they begin to learn how individuals can reason
> clearly about vexing moral issues and choices, and
> what it means to act in morally responsible ways
> consistent with such reasons and choices.[4]

Public schools in a democracy have a duty to teach students to think about what they would otherwise simply take for granted. The task of the schools is to teach them to examine new ideas and to face new questions. Obviously this must be done in ways that are suitable for the age of students, but even young children ask questions.

People who see the schools in this way are often accused of "secular humanism" by their fundamentalist critics, who see it as a do-your-own-thing philosophy that teaches that all values are relative and encourages children to do as they please. In reality, it emphasizes the importance of thinking for oneself, of taking other people seriously, of treating ideas with an open mind and of not being satisfied with easy answers. It does not regard all values as relative but does believe that values should be open to scrutiny. It is a tradition that goes back to the beginnings of civilization. It is central to the idea of liberal education and to the principles of democracy. It is the only tradition of thought that deliberately and continually questions its own fundamental beliefs. Nor is it incompatible with religious faith. As the prominent Roman Catholic educator and philosopher, Cardinal Newman, said in the nineteenth century, "Great minds need elbow room, not indeed in the domain of faith, but of thought. And so indeed do lesser minds and all minds."[5]

This need for intellectual elbow room must be defended in the schools. Parents have the right to withdraw their students from any activity they find unacceptable. They do not have the right to impose their personal opinions on schools, which are supposed to serve the community as a whole. One of the main responsibilities the school has to its community in a democracy is to explore controversial problems with students.

These problems, however, should be those that involve society as a whole. They should be the public issues that citizens have to deal with as citizens, not matters of personal lifestyle and belief. Clearly schools should not be in the business of attacking students' religious beliefs, encouraging premarital sex, condoning drug use, or any other such behaviour. They should, however, be encouraging students to *think* about social and political issues that are controversial in society.

It goes without saying that this should always be done in a tolerant, open way that respects the range of opinions that exists. To say that schools should teach students to explore controversial public issues is not to say they should simply thumb their noses at ideas and beliefs people consider important. But it is an important part of any education worth the name. It will from time to time give rise to controversy, but this is not a reason for not doing it.

As citizens, we are expected to think about and vote on difficult problems, about which people have strong and varied opinions, while always respecting people's right to believe what they choose. There will obviously always be difficult cases. Does freedom of speech permit the sale of pornography? Does political freedom allow racists to state their views publicly? Should certain books be banned from school libraries? Should workers in essential services have the right to strike? Should the local hospital provide abortion services? Should the need to correct gender inequities mean hiring preferences for women over men? Such questions can test the limits of democracy, of our willingness to subject our personal beliefs to the test of public debate, and of our readiness to live with majority decisions we do not particularly like. And school is one of the places, sometimes the only place, where we can learn the skills and habits of mind that allow us to do all this successfully.

For this reason some educators have called for special programs in values education. As they see it, values can easily get lost in the pursuit of subject matter, and they are too important to be left to chance. They must be dealt with either in special courses or by making values education an important part of existing subjects. In recent years, this focus on deliberate values education has taken three forms. One is "values clarification," which seeks to help students become clearer about their personal values, to think about them and consider their implications for everyday life. The second is "values analysis," which teaches students to examine controversial social and political problems, to analyse the beliefs people have about them and to arrive at their own personal positions. The third emphasizes "moral reasoning" and "moral development" and teaches students how to think about difficult problems of right and wrong, justice and fairness.

None of the three approaches teaches students *what* to think about difficult or controversial value questions; they concentrate instead on teaching them *how* to think. As a result, they have met with some opposition. Some critics believe that the schools have absolutely no business dealing with such topics, which belong in the home and are the responsibility of parents, not teachers. Some claim that these approaches to values education undermine the values of home and church. Some see the topics that are dealt with in values education, not as issues or problems at all, but as matters of right and wrong about which there can be no discussion. Some fear that opening up classrooms to such topics will lead, not to open discussion in which all viewpoints are represented, but to propaganda and indoctrination, especially when a teacher has strong personal views.

Perhaps the most serious objection is the one that rejects the whole idea of allowing students to explore controversial problems and insists that the schools should be teaching them absolute standards of right and wrong, though it is not always clear what these standards might be on some of the tough issues that face us. They are issues precisely because they do not have easy answers and people do not agree on what is right or wrong. I used to teach my history students what I called Osborne's first law of politics. It went as follows: "To any political problem there are two solutions; one is bad, the other is worse." My point was that political problems do not have easy solutions. That is precisely why they are political problems. The solution to a political problem is usually a choice of the lesser evil and so is guaranteed to offend some part of the population. That, after all, is the nature of democratic politics.

However they are handled, values play an important part in schooling. We want schools to teach children to behave properly, though we might sometimes disagree about what that means. We want schools to teach the values of work, responsibility, respect for others, and respect for human rights in general. We should also want the schools to teach students how to explore controversial and sensitive value questions. Democracy demands no less.

REFERENCES

1. Robert W. Galvin, Chairman of the Executive Committee, Motorola, & Edward W. Bales, Director of Education—External Systems, Motorola. *Teaching the New Basic Skills: Principles for Educating Children to Thrive in a Changing Economy.* New York: The Free Press, 1996, p. XVII.

2. *People and Skills in the New Global Economy.* Toronto: Premier's Council, 1990, p. 85.

3. *For the Love of Learning: Report of the Royal Commission on Learning.* Toronto: Queen's Printer, 1994, VOL 1, p. 61.

4. *Report of the Royal Commission on Education.* Victoria: British Columbia Department of Education, 1988, p. 70.

5. Martha Nussbaum. *Cultivating Humanity: A Classical Defense of Reform in Liberal Education.* Cambridge: Harvard University Press, 1997, p. 265.

CHAPTER FIVE

One Curriculum or Many?

THE CURRICULUM EXPLOSION

When I began teaching in 1961, most high school students followed the same curriculum. One or two classes were separated out into a "terminal" course, which was given that name because it led to nothing beyond high school. There were also a few classes taking a "commercial" course, though most of their subjects outside the commercial area, such as science, history, English and so on, were the same as those taken by the rest of the school. But most students took the "matriculation" course, which led to university, even though most of them had no university plans. They wanted to keep all their options open and were well aware that university entrance qualifications were needed for most white collar jobs.

Today, in schools across the country, things are very different. Instead of one curriculum taken by most students, there is a smorgasbord of offerings. French immersion, the international baccalaureate, advanced placement, general, vocational, modified, gifted, special needs—the variety is dazzling. And some of these curricula are themselves offered at varying levels of difficulty. No longer do we expect most students to take more or less the same program, consisting of a common core of subjects with a handful of electives thrown in. Today's high schools have been compared to shopping malls where a wide variety of goods (courses) is on offer, with the customers (students) free to choose what they want according to taste. Today students graduate, not by completing an agreed curriculum, but by accumulating the required number of credits. In most cases, these credits have to be chosen within certain limits, so many in science, so many in social studies and so on, but this still leaves students with a wide variety of choices.

High schools created commercial and technical courses in the early 1900s, but the real explosion of curricular choice began in the mid-1960s. Educators believed that many of the students entering high school for the first time in those years would find the existing program too "academic," too abstract or simply too difficult, and therefore needed different curricula, ones that were more practical, more connected with the real world and less "bookish." This move to open up the curriculum was reinforced by the individualized, student-centred philosophy that took hold of education in these years, with its belief in student choice and in fitting the curriculum to the student rather than the student to the curriculum.

Across the country, ministries of education moved to a European model of schooling, offering different curricula to different kinds of students. They set up academic courses for the twenty to thirty percent of students who were thought to be university-bound, technical courses for those interested in the trades, remedial and basic courses for so-called slow learners, and general courses for the fifty to sixty percent of students who were thought to be "average" and probably headed straight for the workforce after they left school. The thinking was that those students who were seriously considering going to university should be given a more demanding program and should not be held back by those students who were not as bright, while the broad mass of average students should not be forced to struggle with work that was too difficult for them.

This model perhaps makes sense on paper, but it breaks down in practice. The central problem is that we simply do not know enough about students to slot them neatly into one program or another. The result is that some students end up getting a much better education than others, not because of any special ability, but because they are lucky enough to be selected for a particular program. I once listened to a high school counsellor explaining to parents of grade nine students which curricula their children should follow when they entered high school. Any students with a 65% average or better in grade nine, he said, should take the academic university entrance curriculum in grade ten. Any students with less than 65%, however, would find this curriculum too difficult and should therefore take the general course. But grade nine marks are simply not accurate enough to be used in this way and students should not find their future determined by what they do in grade nine. All the evidence we have suggests that educational success depends at least as much on home background and social class as it does on raw ability.

Our judgments of what students can do are only informed guesses. Students constantly surprise us. We can never know enough about them to say with certainty and for all time that one student belongs here and another belongs somewhere else. To separate students into different curriculum programs too often closes their options. It forces them into making career decisions before they really need to. It also sets up a grossly unequal school system, in which some students get a first-rate curriculum, but many others do not. This is more than a matter of different curricula running side by side. The minority of students who take the most demanding program often do so at the expense of those who do not. Their good fortune is made possible by everyone else's sacrifice. Teachers commonly report that the departure of the most motivated and talented students into gifted programs, for example, has had the effect of lowering the level of the classes of which they are no longer part. Even a university entrance class will experience a drop in standards if the best students leave for a more academically demanding program.

There is a certain chemistry in a classroom. It can include students of all types, the bright and the not so bright, the hardworking and the lazy, the co-operative and the apathetic, and so on, but often the tone is set by a certain group of students. The presence of a group of highfliers in a class can pull everyone along, so that many students end up doing better than they otherwise might. That has certainly been my experience. Years ago, I taught grade ten classes in British and American history. The classes attracted the more academically interested students. They were, from a teacher's point of view, good students and officially described as "university entrance." Every year, however, the school administration asked me to take a few students who needed to finish their grade ten year and who had run out of options. They were good people but not good students, and were officially labelled not as "university entrance" but as "general." I took them in, and rather than creating a special set of "general level" activities for them, treated them the same way I treated the rest of the class. They did the same assignments, the same amount of reading and essay writing, and so forth.

Something interesting happened. Rather than floundering or failing, they rose to the level of the class. They were never in the top ranks and I saw no miraculous transformations, but they got passing marks, honestly earned, with no special favours from me. I had and have only two explanations. One, the class set a certain tone, a certain level of performance, and this pulled everyone along. Two, as a teacher I expected these students to do well, or at least well enough to pass, and they responded. And there is a solid body of research that suggests that, within some obvious limits, teachers' expectations influence students' performance.

This is one of the negative results of the separation of curricula that exploded in the 1960s. When teachers know that they are teaching a "general" level class, it is dangerously easy for them to lower their expectations. The thinking, which is often unconscious, goes like this: these are general level students, they are not academic material, they will not read much, they write with difficulty, they might create discipline problems, therefore I had better keep them occupied with lots of busywork. Instead of writing essays, they write only paragraphs, and often not even that, being required only to fill in the blanks on prepared worksheets. Rather than being required to read a variety of books, they are expected, at most, to grind though the textbook. As for homework, forget it. It is what Ontario educationist Bob Davis calls, in his book *What Our High Schools Could Be* the "numbing and dumbing" approach to teaching.

Students themselves play along. Knowing they have been labelled "general," they see no reason to exert themselves. If the school has, in a certain sense, given up on them as far as academic work is concerned, it is understandable that they decide to give up on the school. After a few years of low-level work, they genuinely do find academic work difficult, or at least uninteresting. They decide to play the system. As my general level students told me on occasion "I can't do this—I'm a general course student." And at first, they often could *not* do what I set them, but they could with some help, practice and lots of work. What they lacked most often was not ability or intelligence but skills and confidence. As Herb Kohl puts it in his book *I Won't Learn from You*, when they failed, it was not for lack of ability but for lack of desire to learn what the school had to teach.

In the early 1960s there were always students who were in danger of failing their courses. As teachers, we knew they might have a tough time passing the provincial examinations. As a result, we laid on extra classes. Usually these were nothing more than cram sessions where we would train students to answer the kinds of questions they would probably find on the examination. But the result was that many of them got their credit. With the introduction of multiple curricula after the mid-1960s, however, the common reaction was not to figure out what had to be done to get students through, but to assume that the course was too difficult for them and direct them into a less demanding program.

The result is today's sequence of curricula streamed in order of difficulty and designed to meet students' needs. It was done for the most humane reasons, but it has condemned too many students to a second-rate program. If I had to choose, I would return to the model that existed when I began teaching, in which most students followed the same curriculum. The highfliers would not get the bells and whistles of the international baccalaureate or advanced placement, but they would still get a good education, and their presence in regular classes would help pull less talented students along.

This is not to say that all students must take the same program, identical in every detail. The Radwanski Report in Ontario in 1987 did favour this, going as far as to recommend that all vocational programs be scrapped. However, we do not need to abolish vocational or other courses, but to rethink them. Too often we have offered students in such programs an inferior version of what education should be, not in their specifically technical courses but in the so-called academic courses they also have to take. In Manitoba, vocational students do not have to take Canadian history, although all other students do. In many parts of the country they get a reduced level of English, mathematics and science. But vocational students will be citizens as well as workers, and all students have the right to make as much of their lives as possible.

All students should take a core of courses that are, in general terms the same for everyone. Such, in fact, is the general direction taken by recent royal commissions on education in British Columbia, New Brunswick and Ontario. All students, regardless of program, should take more or less the same version of history, English, the sciences and so forth. In Canada they should also study both official languages. There are plenty of school systems around the

world where it is taken for granted that all students should learn a
second language. It should not be impossible in an officially bilingual
country such as Canada.

STREAMING

To SUGGEST THAT MOST students should take more or less the same
program, or at least the same core courses, and that all curricula
should present the same level of challenge, raises the question of
streaming (sometimes called tracking). This is the term used to
describe the process of sorting students into different programs
according to ability, interest or future plans. All schools do it at the
high school level, but its influence reaches down into the early
grades.

The political left has long opposed streaming, seeing it as a way
of keeping working class and minority students out of challenging
programs and therefore giving them an inferior education. In broad
terms, it creates two kinds of students: those who are thought to be
academic and those who are not. Students in the second group are
thought to be more interested in so-called "practical" learning than
in books. They are also often thought to be less intelligent and less
interested in school.

In recent years this division between academic and non-
academic has been questioned in Canada, as has the whole practice
of streaming. In 1987 the Radwanksi Report described streaming as
a social injustice, a theoretical error and a practical failure. Radwanski was no flaming radical. He had been instructed to investigate
why students dropped out of high school, and he found that for the
most part they dropped out because they had given up on school.
Why? Because they had been shunted into dead-end programs that
gave them no hope and no interest in schooling. They had been
streamed out of anything resembling a decent education. In 1988
the British Columbia Royal Commission on Education reached the
same conclusion as Radwanski, as did the New Brunswick Commission on Education of 1993 and Ontario's Royal Commission on
Learning in 1994. They all found that streaming worked against students who were not placed in university entrance courses.

The only students who benefit from streaming are those placed
in the top classes, where they receive a challenging curriculum taught
in interesting ways, often by a school's most qualified teachers. It is

not the fact of streaming in and of itself that makes these classes so successful, but the quality of teaching students receive once they have been streamed and the way they respond to it. It is hardly surprising that a class of excellent students, taught by specially qualified teachers following a special curriculum, should prove successful.

Unfortunately, as we saw earlier, their removal from regular classes lowers the performance of those who are left behind. At the same time, students in lower streams get less interesting and challenging work. They present more discipline problems for teachers, who lower their expectations, and students, in turn, work down to what is expected of them. A vicious circle sets in.

Their low performance, however, has very little to do with ability. Lower stream students are not stupid or lacking intelligence. They are turned off school. They do not possess the skills and attitudes that give them a head start in schooling. Above all, they are often close to or below the poverty line, so that they and their parents face far more more urgent problems than what to do about school. As a result, these students slip back year by year, until by high school it seems that the only choice is to assign them to a low program stream.

The research is overwhelming: wherever streaming is used, middle-class students go into the higher streams, and working-class students into the lower. Unless one assumes that most working-class students are naturally stupid and most middle-class students are naturally bright, the conclusion is obvious: streaming reflects not intelligence or ability but social class. Which is also why so many minority students are found in the lower streams. Streaming not only reflects social class divisions, it strengthens them. It not only effectively excludes many working-class youngsters from a challenging education, but does so in ways that make it appear to be their own fault.

If streaming is such a disaster for so many students, and the research leaves little doubt that it is, the question naturally arises: Why do we do it? As with most things, the answer can be found in history.

As more and more students began to go to high school, beginning in the early 1900s, but especially since the 1960s, educators assumed that the existing curriculum would be too difficult for most of them. It was intended to prepare students for university, not for jobs, but most students did not intend to go to university. Schooling had to be made more "practical." Latin and Greek were replaced by shorthand, bookkeeping and technical drawing; history became social studies. Subjects were reorganized to prepare students less for university and more for the "real world." It seemed to make sense to organize a variety of programs according to what students planned to do after they left school. Some would go on to university. Some would go to trade school or apprenticeship. Some would go straight into the workforce. Each group, it was believed, deserved its own kind of program.

It was also believed that people had different levels of intelligence and ability. By the 1920s psychologists and guidance counsellors believed that the newly developed intelligence and aptitude tests could slot students into the programs best suited to them.

If students were different in ability and intelligence, it seemed to make sense to teach them differently. Bright students could do more demanding work than average ones. They wrote essays and research papers; the rest wrote paragraphs or filled out worksheets. They organized debates and projects; the rest filled in the questions at the end of the chapter. They read books, and lots of them; the rest struggled with the textbook. They could work with their minds; the rest only with their hands. They could think and reason; the rest had to learn to follow instructions. They were destined to become leaders; the rest followers.

Educators saw this as humane and rational. In their view, it was both cruel and inefficient to make students suffer in a program that was too difficult for them. But though educators acted from the best of motives, the result was that the public school system became a vast sieve, sorting out students according to what society was thought to need.

When the economy was such that students could leave school with few or no skills and still find decent and secure jobs, streaming was more or less taken for granted. But in an economy where, we are told, skills are ever more necessary, streaming is no longer acceptable. For those who believe that the main task of the schools is not to train workers but to educate children to become good citizens and to make the most of their lives, it never was.

Streaming is not just a school issue, it is a question of social justice. We should not accept a system that so easily gives so many students a less challenging education than they deserve. In one sense we recognize this, which is why in recent years we have "mainstreamed" special-needs students into regular classes. We realized that to segregate such students was to assign them to a lower quality of education. But we have not yet recognized that academic streaming does this on a far larger scale.

The answer to streaming, however, is not simply to throw a group of students into the same classroom and then tell teachers to make the best of it, as has too often been the case with mainstreaming students with special needs. In 1991 Ontario announced that it was going to "destream" grade nine, and many teachers complained bitterly. At about the same time, Manitoba announced its intention to "destream" grade ten English and geography (interestingly, not science or mathematics) and met with the same kind of protest. As teachers see it, destreaming can only make their work more difficult. To destream schools will involve more fundamental reforms than simply putting students together in the same class.

DO WE NEED A NATIONAL CURRICULUM?

SOME CRITICS OF THE schools would like the curriculum to be the same right across the country. As they see it, a national curriculum would establish uniform standards throughout Canada, raise standards generally, make it possible to use the best brains in the country to develop programs regardless of province, promote national unity, help children settle into schools if they move from province to province and eliminate the duplication and overlap that exist with each province developing its own curriculum. It is not a new idea. In the 1890s, especially in Ontario and the West, the idea of a common course in Canadian history was popular. If all students everywhere studied the same history, so it was believed, national unity would be strengthened. A prize was offered to anyone who wrote a national history textbook that would be fair to all parts of the country. Someone actually won it, but the book was rejected in most provinces. This example tells us something: however attractive the idea of national curriculum looks on paper, it is almost certain that it will be rejected by some of the provinces.

Canada is one of the very few countries in the world without a national ministry of education. Even the United States, which prides itself on its tradition of local control of education, has a federal office of education that sponsors research, gives out grants and generally concerns itself with education policy. We have nothing like this in Canada. Nor, given our history, are we likely to have, though the 1993 Newfoundland and Labrador Royal Commission on Education recommended the creation of a national office of education that would set national goals and standards, organize national testing and assessment, and sponsor research. The Ontario Royal Commission in 1994 was far more cautious, saying the idea was worth exploring but unlikely to achieve the results some people expected. It argued that a national curriculum would not necessarily improve the quality of schooling, but would definitely open up an enormous constitutional debate.

The provinces and territories are unwilling to give up their constitutional control of education. They are prepared to co-operate, but only on their own terms; they certainly will not tolerate being told what to to do by Ottawa. There is an interprovincial group, the Council of Ministers of Education Canada, with a small permanent staff, that serves as a national organization, though it can do only what the provinces and territories allow it to do. In recent years there has been an increasing amount of interprovincial co-operation, especially in the exchange of information, research, testing of students and most recently in curriculum development.

The supporters of a national curriculum argue that the countries that consistently do well on international tests of students, notably Japan and some European countries, have national curricula, and that, if Canada were to follow their lead, our educational performance would improve. But the argument is not all that convincing. Many countries that do *poorly* on international tests also have national curricula. In the case of countries like Japan, it is not the existence of a national curriculum but what happens in the classroom that is important.

Though we do not have a national curriculum, there is already a fair amount of similarity in curricula and textbooks across Canada. Moreover, the Council of Ministers of Education Canada is now sponsoring regional curriculum development. The four western provinces and the territories are now developing common standards in all the major subjects of the curriculum. Unless the provinces are prepared to give up their control of education, creating a national curriculum and a national office of education would simply add another level of bureaucracy to an already top-heavy educational system.

More than anything else, however, any serious attempt to introduce a national curriculum in Canada would raise so many constitutional and political difficulties that the dust would probably never settle. And since there is no guarantee that simply developing a national curriculum would produce any noticeable result, it is best to let sleeping dogs lie. We should concentrate our efforts on improving what we have, not trying to do the impossible.

Part 3

Teachers and Teaching

CHAPTER SIX

What is Good Teaching?

THE IMPORTANCE OF TEACHING

A CURRICULUM CAN ONLY ever be as good as the teacher who is teaching it. The best curriculum in the world will never be more than a piece of paper until teachers turn it into something that will help students learn. As we have seen, teachers adapt their teaching to what they think their students need. If they think the curriculum does not serve their students well or is unteachable, they will give up on it and do something else. If any curriculum is to work, teachers must agree that it makes sense, that it is workable and that it will help students.

Even when teachers do follow the curriculum, they influence students in many ways. They can lead students either to love or hate a subject and, much more important, to love or hate learning itself. More than this, teachers can shape the way students see themselves. Children are not born good or bad students. This is something they learn. Those who do well at school learn to like it. In a thousand different ways they get the message that they are good students, and that is how they quickly come to define themselves. On the other hand, students who find school difficult soon learn to dislike it. Their marks, their teachers' comments, their being put in slow groups, their problems in understanding what they are taught, or even seeing the point of it, all combine to identify them not as bad children but as poor students. And once they are identified this way, they often act accordingly, so that by about grade four, if not sooner, their future in school is more or less decided. Falling further and further behind, by high school they end up in the low-stream programs—when they do not drop out altogether. Their test scores, and often their general attitude to school, make it almost inevitable.

We used to think that this separating of students was the result of intelligence and ability. It seems obvious that some people are born with more brains than others and therefore will do better at school. Indeed, many people believe that one of the duties of schools is to sort out the bright from the not-so-bright and teach them accordingly, which is why we give so much attention to students we believe to be gifted or talented. It seems ridiculous to think that the great majority of students can successfully take more or less the same program.

Ridiculous or not, however, researchers are now saying that they can, provided we are willing to rethink what we do in schools. For one thing, psychologists are giving us a clearer picture of what we mean by intelligence and academic ability, which is something to be discussed in the next chapter. For another, schoolwork is not so difficult that it is beyond the grasp of most people. The problem is that people learn at different rates and in different ways, whereas schools often operate as though we learn in only one way and all at the same speed. A student's achievement in school is as much a matter of attitude and effort as it is of ability or intelligence. We too easily see students' mistakes as signs that their work might be too difficult for them and so we lower our expectations accordingly. Japanese teachers, on the other hand, see mistakes as signs not of a lack of ability but of difficulties in understanding that can be overcome with hard work. They do not lower their expectations of students; rather, they rethink their teaching.

What students do in school is, at least in part, a result of what their teachers expect of them. In an experiment in the 1960s, researchers told teachers that twenty percent of students in their classes had been identified as gifted and that they were interested in following their progress. In reality, the students had been selected totally at random, and were neither brighter nor slower than anyone else. Nonetheless, after a year of schooling, not only had they done unusually well in school, but their IQ scores had increased. The research led to only one conclusion: when teachers expected students to do well, they did so.

Other experiments have produced similar findings with respect to behaviour. In one of them, a grade six teacher in the United States wanted to give her students an understanding of prejudice. To do this, she divided her class into blue-eyed and brown-eyed groups and treated them very differently. For example, when blue-eyed students did something wrong or made a mistake, they were treated gently and shown how to do better, but when brown-eyed students did the same thing, the teacher made it clear she did not expect anything better from them. In addition, she gave one group clear privileges over the other, for example, in her handling of washroom breaks, of trips to the water fountain, of seating arrangements and so on. She found that rather than seeing the whole exercise as a game, the blue-eyed students very quickly came to believe that they were indeed a superior breed, and the brown-eyes equally quickly saw themselves as inferior—so inferior, in fact, that they believed they deserved the second-rate treatment they were getting.[1]

Such experiments show how easily students respond to what is expected of them. But it is a more complicated business than that, for simply expecting students to do well does not mean they automatically will. Teachers show what they expect in many different ways, often without realizing themselves what they are doing. It may be a word or a gesture, a response to a student's question, a tone of voice, or a way of correcting a student's mistake. If students who are expected to do well make a mistake or have difficulty, a teacher will often take the time to work with them, but without in any way lowering the standard of work expected. When, on the other hand, students who are expected to do badly make mistakes, it is dangerously easy for teachers to assume that this is a sign of their lack of intelligence and to lower their standards by assigning work that they judge the students can handle.

It is not that teachers deliberately play favourites or are prejudiced against certain kinds of students, but that they set different expectations for different students. They view intelligence as a fixed quantity that students have more or less of, so that some find schoolwork easy and others hard. At the same time, teachers realize perfectly well that what students do in school is often a result of influences beyond their control. Children who live in poverty, and that is about a fifth of Canadian children these days, often have more difficulty in school than those whose families are well off. However, teachers have neither the time nor the resources to give such children the help they need.

The school system is not flexible enough to let them do so. Students have to complete a given amount of work in a given grade, regardless of how quickly or slowly they learn. In these circumstances, it is not surprising that, rather than failing children on test after test and assignment after assignment, and so turning them against school completely, teachers lower their standards so that everyone can have some taste of success. This is why, for example, for so many years elementary classes were arranged in groups of robins, sparrows and bluebirds, and why high schools offer different program streams, all according to what teachers believe to be the ability of students, but all serving to create and reinforce different expectations, not only in the minds of teachers but in the minds of students.

Teachers are important in students' lives in other ways. They can serve as examples of learning in action, of people who see learning as enjoyable, exciting, worth pursuing in its own right. They can also widen students' horizons by introducing them to experiences and ideas that might otherwise never have occurred to them. Here is a description of one such teacher in a grade five classroom:

> Every day in class we listened to classical music and looked at classical or modern paintings. She read from novels to open the day and usually closed the day with a poem. I didn't understand or like most of what she presented to us, but I didn't resist it since I could see that she put her whole being into her presentations. She hummed with the music, would tell us to listen to the violins or the trumpets, would repeat a line or two of poetry several times, almost singing it. And she told us not not to bother trying to like or understand what she exposed us to, just to open ourselves up and listen and look. She explained that she was just planting seeds and that it would take time for them to grow in us.[2]

Teachers are important for more than academic reasons. They often serve as advisers, mentors and guides to students on just about every aspect of their lives. It is not unusual to hear adults who achieve some honour pay tribute to a teacher who inspired or encouraged them. Teachers can be the first people to spot that something needs fixing in a student's life. This is why, for example, they are now obligated to report even a suspicion of child abuse to the appropriate authorities. Working with parents, and even without them in some cases, they can shape students' futures.

Teachers are also expected to serve as models of how to behave and how to live, which is one reason their private lives are sometimes in the spotlight. Religious schools often impose strict standards of conduct on their teachers. Public schools are more tolerant, but even they have certain limits. It was not so long ago that teachers were not supposed to drink in public, appear pregnant in the classroom or in any way to flout the standards of the community.

A teacher's values and beliefs can sometimes raise difficult questions. We would prefer not to have racists teaching our children, and in recent years teachers have been removed from the classroom for their racist beliefs. Such teachers usually defend themselves by appealing to the right of free speech in a democracy, and by arguing that they keep their beliefs out of the classroom. Their opponents respond that free speech has limits and that, even if teachers are able to keep their beliefs out of the classroom, the fact that they are known to hold these beliefs and promote them outside the classroom still has an influence on children. Most of us would agree, but nonetheless feel a nagging doubt about where the lines should be drawn. At the height of the Cold War in the 1950s and 1960s, teachers were sometimes dismissed if they were thought to be Communists. Should teachers' private values or political beliefs automatically disqualify them from teaching? Or should teachers be judged strictly on the basis of their competence in the classroom? Whatever the answer, there can be no doubt that we expect teachers to serve as good examples for our children.

All of which raises the question: What is good teaching and how do we obtain it?

WHAT DEFINES A GOOD TEACHER?

THIS SEEMS TO BE an easy question until we try to answer it. Much obviously depends on what we mean by the word "good." Does it mean getting students through their examinations? Helping them feel good about themselves? Introducing them to new ideas?

Preparing them for jobs? Making sure they are ready for the next grade of schooling? Helping them deal with some problem they face in their lives? Or some combination of all of these things?

There can be no single formula for good teaching. It cannot be reduced to a set of rules, though this has not stopped people from trying. I was once told by a principal that no teacher who was any good lectured to students for more than twenty minutes, since after that time students simply tuned out. Perhaps so, but it all depends on the circumstances. I have seen quite young students transfixed by a film or a good story for over an hour. Teaching is too complex to be reduced to a set of hard-and-fast rules in this way. Nonetheless, there are various "models" of good teaching that try to reduce teaching to a set of specified things a teacher must do in a lesson.

In reality good teaching can be defined only in very general terms. To talk about it is like describing a good hockey forward as someone who scores goals or makes plays, without specifying exactly how this is to be done. The 1994 Ontario Royal Commission on Learning defined good teaching as follows:

1. Teachers care about their students and their learning, and know them well enough to teach them effectively.
2. Teachers know their subjects and know how to teach so that students understand them.
3. Teachers are guided by clear goals and successfully organize and manage students' learning.
4. Teachers work with others, including colleagues, parents and the community in general.
5. Teachers continually think about what they do and continue to learn throughout their careers.[3]

The main problem with such assumptions is that they reduce teaching to a set of neutral techniques that say nothing about the value of what is being taught. James Keegstra, the Alberta teacher who taught his students that the Holocaust was a hoax and that the world was controlled by a vast Jewish conspiracy, was able to get away with this nonsense for years because he was considered a good teacher. Judged in terms of pure technique, he apparently was. His lessons were well prepared and organized, he worked well with students and he was conscientious. On checklists of good teaching he scored well. The problem was that no one assessed the content of what he was actually teaching. But no attempt to define good teaching can be separated from questions of goals and values in this way. Good teaching involves *what* as well as *how* we teach.

There are many descriptions of good teaching available and they all say much the same thing. One, good teachers know their subjects thoroughly, have a wide general knowledge besides, and genuinely enjoy learning as well as teaching. Two, they make what they know understandable and interesting to students. Three, they have a wide repertoire of teaching techniques and understand how students learn and think, while also getting to know well the particular students they are responsible for teaching. Four, they strike a balance between maintaining their authority and control and being open and accessible to students. Five, they enjoy the respect and confidence of their students by being organized, fair, consistent, flexible within limits, willing to listen but also willing to establish clear and reasonable rules and expectations. Six, they work with parents and any other people who can help them advance their students' education. Seven, they are always ready to think about the way they work and to reconsider their ideas and beliefs.

TEACHING METHODS

GOOD TEACHERS USE A wide variety of teaching methods. They know that students learn in different ways and so benefit from different approaches to teaching. Moreover, most students, whatever their style of learning, appreciate some variety in their lessons. School can too easily become a prolonged experience of being talked at.

Teaching methods carry their own message. Students can learn that they do not know very much and even that they are stupid, that their job is to learn what their teachers put in front of them and that they must obey authority and follow orders. This can be done cruelly or humanely, but either way, the message is one of conformity and dependence. Alternatively, students can learn that they are intelligent, that what they know matters, that they know more than they realize, that although there is much they do not know they are capable of learning it and that discussion, questioning and criticism are important parts of learning.

Depending on the teacher's choice of teaching methods, students can learn that learning, and perhaps life itself, is a matter of

competing against others, of second-guessing what people in authority expect (hence that frequent classroom question "Will this be on
the test?"), that success means outsmarting others, that there are
winners and losers, and that what matters is to be a winner. Or they
can learn that learning means co-operating with others, that many
heads are usually better than one, that learning means sharing ideas,
offering one's ideas for comment and criticism, that effort and per-
sistence can pay off and that success is the result of hard work more
than of native ability.

Consider the problem of teaching grade seven students about
the ancient Greek city-state. The conventional approach is to walk
students through the textbook, perhaps look for a story or two to
add interest, show a filmstrip, assign questions. It is sometimes
described as the transmission method of teaching. It can be done
efficiently and, if done by a good teacher, can interest students. But
its message to students is that here is something they do not
know, but their teacher does, that everything they need to know is
to be found in the textbook or the teacher's notes, that there are no
unanswered questions or unsolved puzzles, that they do not have to
concern themselves with how we know anything at all about ancient
Greece or with the deeper question of why they have to study the
topic at all, that what they already know has nothing to do with
school, and that to learn something means to be able to answer
somebody else's questions.

A livelier approach that sends a very different message to students begins with what they already know. The teacher begins, for
example, by asking them about hermits and using their answers to
raise the question of why most people choose to live not alone but
together. This leads to a consideration of the advantages of living in
groups rather than alone. In my experience, students offer a rich
variety of suggestions, and on this basis, the teacher then leads the
students to think about two kinds of groups, crowds and communities, and what distinguishes one from the other. Drawing on their
own general knowledge, the students quickly understand that a
crowd is a collection of people gathered in one place for a short
period of time, while a community is based on shared beliefs and
values and is much longer lasting. The teacher then leads them to
think about whether their class is a community, or their school, or
their neighbourhood. Using all this discussion, most of which
comes from the students in response to the teacher's prompts and

questions, the teacher then introduces the ancient Greek city-states, explaining that these were a form of community that were in some ways similar to, and in some ways very different from, the way we live today. The students then move on to a study of the Greek city-state, with their final activity being a comparison between the ancient city-states and their own town.

Here, as in the first approach, the students learn history, but they also learn that what they already know is important, that history is not only to be memorized but to be understood and questioned, that what happened in the distant past has something to tell us today, and above all, that to learn means to think, to share ideas, to push what they know to its limits and beyond; in a word, that they are intelligent.

Unfortunately this approach to teaching remains the exception rather than the rule. When it is used, it is often considered suitable only for so-called gifted or academic students, despite the fact that when used with so-called slower or non-academic students, it usually proves they are not so slow after all.

I used to use a set of about ten slides with grade seven and eight history classes showing different British castles. I began by asking the students to tell me exactly what they saw; their answers were straightforward, although I sometimes had to fish for details they had either overlooked or taken for granted. What they saw included high towers, battlements, thick walls, castles built on high ground or cliffs, castles overshadowing villages and towns, and so on. My next questions dealt with how, if they had been soldiers at the time, they would have attacked these castles. My questions were always anchored in the slides so that the students were always faced with a specific problem—not how would you attack castles in general, but how would you attack this particular building in this particular place? Usually they came up with all the actual techniques of medieval warfare and sometimes added a few of their own devising. Their suggestions had to be realistic: spaceships and death rays were ruled out, as were guns and other modern weapons. Their answers included ladders to scale the walls, catapults to batter the fortifications from afar, mass attacks to saturate the defence, tunnelling to collapse the walls, siege to starve out the defenders, and sometimes even bribery.

I pursued each of these suggestions in detail. If the favoured method of attack was tunnelling, my questions included: Where would you begin the tunnel? Where would you find the labour? How would you make sure it went where it was supposed to go? How would you dispose of the earth? How would you prevent the tunnel from collapsing on the men digging it? How would you plan the tunnel so that it actually would collapse the castle wall? Students always came up with reasonable answers to these questions, but one final question usually gave them pause for thought. How would you cause the tunnel to collapse in the right way at the right time so as to undermine the walls above it and not trap any of the tunnellers. Usually their answers involved a complicated system of ropes tied to the timber props that supported the tunnel, all of which would be pulled away at the same time. It was not difficult to show them that this was extremely difficult to do and too complicated to be successful. Further questioning usually brought them to the solution used by medieval miners: coat the props in some flammable material, set fire to the whole thing (people would have enough time to do this and still get out of the tunnel before it collapsed) and then wait for results.

Having taken the students though the ways of attacking castles, I switched gears and asked them how they would build castles to protect them from attack, still using the slides as a framework for discussion. Students always proved equal to the task. Assault by ladder could be defended against by building walls and towers too high to be scaled. Head-on attack could be turned back by making sure there was enough open space around the castle walls to provide a killing ground that attackers could not cross. Attempts to use battering rams could be blocked by making the ground floor of a tower nothing but solid earth.

Finally, having brought out all the information, I asked the students to organize it under headings and subheadings, so that they made and organized their own notes. In the space of a lesson or two students covered the possibilities of attack and defence, and almost everything came from their own heads.

As in the example of the Greek city-states, they learned more than history. They found out that they knew more than they thought and that schoolwork was open to exploration and imagination. Rather than being presented with factual information, which they simply had to memorize and repeat, they came up with the information themselves, organized it and summarized it, and in the process remembered it more effectively.

I rarely found a class where the students were not full of ideas and suggestions, sometimes realistic and sometimes not, but always full of originality and thought. And I usually found that "slower" classes were just as forthcoming and bright as their supposedly more academic counterparts and sometimes more so. "Good" students can be so afraid of offering a wrong answer that they are reluctant to speak up, whereas "slow" students, once their attention is caught, are prepared to take risks. There is a good deal of truth in the argument of some researchers that what separates good students from bad ones is not intelligence but a willingness to play the school game. Academic students are willing to go along with their teachers, to answer all kinds of questions, to do whatever they are asked and then some. As a result, they are labelled bright and treated accordingly. Non-academic students, on the other hand, often see less point in what they are asked to do and as a result do it badly or not at all. And so, bit by bit, they are reduced to filling in the blanks on worksheets, colouring pictures, reading the textbook aloud and doing other forms of educational donkey-work.

TEACHING BY TELLING

THE TRADITIONAL VIEW OF teaching sees it as the transmission of knowledge, skills and values, a one-way sending of a message from the expert to a novice, in which the receiver's job is to take in the message as accurately as possible. It is a tradition with a long history and was greatly strengthened with the creation of public schooling. There were things that all students were required to know and be able to do, and teachers were therefore required to teach the officially approved curriculum, from beginning to end.

In this view of teaching, students needed only to be filled up with their teachers' knowledge. As long ago as 1854, Charles Dickens attacked it in his novel, *Hard Times*, with his portrayal of Mr. Gradgrind and his philosophy of Facts: "Teach these boys and girls nothing but Facts. Facts alone are wanted in life. Plant nothing else. You can only form the minds of reasoning animals upon Facts; nothing else will ever be of service to them." Visiting his school, Gradgrind asked the students to describe a horse. One of them, Sissy Jupe, could not answer to his satisfaction, so he called on another student who gave him the answer he was looking for: "Quadruped. Gramnivorous. Forty teeth, namely twenty-four grinders, four eye-teeth, and twelve incisive. Sheds coat in the spring; in marshy countries sheds hoofs too. Hoofs hard, but requiring to be shod with iron. Age known by marks in mouth."

Dicken's point was that Sissy Jupe could have described a horse perfectly well in her own words. Her father worked in a circus and she lived with horses on a daily basis. However, she could not meet Mr. Gradgrind's particular demand for "Facts." As Dickens put it, she and the rest of the class were "little pitchers" waiting to be filled with facts. To make his point even clearer, Dickens went on to describe the teacher hired by Mr. Gradgrind, the revealingly named Mr. M'Choakumchild:

> He and some one hundred forty other schoolmasters had been lately turned at the same time, in the same factory, on the same principles, like so many pianoforte legs. He had been put through an immense variety of paces, and had answered volumes of head-breaking questions. Orthography, etymology, syntax, prosody, biography, astronomy, geography, and general cosmography, the sciences of compound proportion, algebra, land-surveying and levelling, vocal music, and drawing from models, were all at the ends of his ten chilled fingers.

After listing many more of Mr. M'Choakumchild's accomplishments, Dickens concluded: "Ah, rather overdone M'Choakumchild! If he had only learnt a little less, how infinitely better he might have taught much more!"

TEACHING BY INQUIRY

EVEN IN 1854 DICKEN'S point was far from new. There has always been an alternative to the view of teaching as transmission. Perhaps its oldest-known description comes from ancient Greece, where Plato describes the philosopher, Socrates, teaching a slave boy. Socrates saw teaching not as putting something into a student, but as pulling out and refining what was already there. He described the teacher as a midwife. He showed that the slave boy, apparently ignorant and certainly uneducated, could, if the teacher asked the right questions, work out for himself some complicated principles of geometry.

Though this view of teaching never won majority support, it never died. Today it is usually described as teaching through inquiry or discovery. In the words of the psychologist Jerome Bruner, it "generally involves not so much the process of leading students to discover what is 'out there' but, instead, their discovering what is in their own heads. It involves encouraging them to say, let me stop and think about that; let me use my head; let me have some vicarious trial and error."[4] Bruner described a grade six lesson to illustrate his point. The class was studying the geography of the northeastern United States. Instead of presenting the students with information, the teacher gave them an outline map showing the main physical features and resources of the region and asking them where they thought people would live. In coming up with their answers, the students provided a wealth of ideas and suggestions, and finally compared their choices with the actual location of the major towns and cities. As in the examples of the Greek city-states and the castles, they not only learned a good deal of factual information, but they also learned to think and to question, and to develop some confidence in their ability to do so.

In 1968, reporting on his investigation of the teaching of Canadian history across the country, A.B. Hodgetts said that the best classes he and his investigators saw in action were those where teachers used an inquiry approach. In these classes teachers rarely lectured and never gave notes or used question-and-answer worksheets. Instead, students read carefully prepared materials ahead of class. These materials gave them whatever factual information they needed to know, presented them with differing interpretations and viewpoints, and raised questions that needed to be pursued. In class, under the direction of their teacher, students discussed the materials, more often talking to one another than to the teacher. At the same time, the teacher kept control of the lesson, asking questions where necessary, adding information, correcting mistakes and generally maintaining the flow of the discussion. In all these classes, students were pursuing a topic in depth, learning whatever facts they needed to know, but going far beyond them in pursuit of questions and ideas. The lessons were, in fact, organized as questions or ideas to be investigated, not, as is so often the case in history, as facts to be covered.

What makes Hodgetts's observations particularly interesting is that less than half of these classes consisted of so-called above-average or academic students. He reported that the method was successful with all kinds of students, including those who were thought to be non-academic or lacking in ability. He urged teachers to abandon the idea that low-ability classes could do only low-level work, noting, "As long as the students in this type of class are taught by hastily designed, dull exposition methods based on the assumption that 'you can't do much with these kids anyway,' they will continue to be unmotivated, uninterested and difficult."[5] As I found in the case of the Greek city-state and medieval castles, this approach to teaching is not only more interesting, for both teachers and students, it appeals to a wide variety of students, often uncovering abilities that neither the students nor their teachers knew they had. Which, in its way, is also the lesson of Socrates—showing 2500 years ago that an apparently ignorant slave boy could do geometry.

There are many variations of transmission and inquiry, but they represent the two major approaches to teaching. Both can be done well or badly. Dickens obviously described a horrendous example of transmission teaching, but a good story, well told, deserves a place in any teacher's repertoire, as does an interesting and question-raising lecture. At the same time, inquiry lessons can easily collapse in chaos if they are not carefully prepared and managed. Of the two approaches, inquiry teaching is much harder to do. It demands a deeper understanding of subject matter, greater flexibility, more careful preparation and a more developed ability to think on one's feet than the much more ordered and prepackaged transmission method. Study after study of schools has shown that only a minority of teachers use inquiry methods, while most rely on transmission, though not with the relentless enthusiasm of Dickens's Mr. Gradgrind.

DIRECT INSTRUCTION OR CHILD-CENTRED TEACHING?

EVEN SO, SOME CRITICS of the schools are now calling for more "direct instruction." In their view, teachers have become too happy-go-lucky. Rather than teaching in the good old-fashioned way, they allow their students too much freedom, favour aimless group work over more formal teaching and generally make too few demands of their students. Teachers, they say, have fallen for the false claims of "child-centred instruction." I once gave a talk to a group of parents and afterwards some of them came up to me to say that I was obviously in favour of child-centred teaching. I replied that of course I was. After all, any teacher has to ensure that what he or she is teaching is centred on students. I discovered, however, that that was not what my critics had in mind. To them child-centred teaching meant no curriculum, no standards, no evaluation, no subject matter, nothing but letting children do what they want and making sure they feel good about themselves, though no teacher I know favours this, and nothing I have read about child-centred teaching supports it.

Teachers obviously have to ensure that what they are teaching makes sense to students. Teaching has to result in learning, or it is not teaching. All teachers have to be child-centred, but they also have to be subject-centred at the same time. It is wrong to contrast subject-centred teaching with child-centred teaching. They are two sides of the same coin. Any halfway competent teacher has to be both. There is an old saying in teaching that runs, "I don't teach subjects, I teach children," but it never made much sense to me. A teacher inevitably teaches subjects, or subject matter, to children. The secret of good teaching is to know how to do it. We should not draw too sharp a line between transmission teaching and inquiry teaching. Good teachers use both, often so intricately mixed that it is not easy to tell which is which.

Critics of child-centred teaching seem to believe that the solution to all classroom problems is to be found in "direct instruction," which requires teachers to teach the whole class as a unit, to use lecture and other direct methods, to assign students lots of drill and seat-work, and to keep everyone working at a uniform rate.

Researchers have found that in some situations direct instruction is the most effective form of teaching, especially when students are expected to learn basic skills, say, in reading or arithmetic, and especially in the elementary grades. At the same time, the researchers caution against making too much of their results. They point out that the research has dealt only with the elementary grades, and that we do not know whether or to what extent direct instruction is effective in the high school. They also point out that the research deals with only one kind of teaching and says nothing about such goals as teaching students to think critically, to work together and so on. It is not a call to put students back in desks and seated in rows, all ready to follow the instructions of the teacher to the letter.

Despite these cautions, some critics of the schools view direct instruction as the solution to everything they see wrong in the schools.

They claim it will raise standards, boost learning, restore authority and generally turn students into productive and responsible citizens. In the same sweeping way, opponents of direct instruction see it as an attempt to turn the classroom into a form of military boot camp and therefore something to be resisted to the last breath. Against direct instruction, they raise the banner of "co-operative learning," an approach that puts students into carefully organized groups, taking on carefully organized tasks and, in many ways, under the supervision of their teachers, teaching each other. Just to confuse matters, research also shows that this can be a very effective way of teaching.

As is often the case, what could be a useful and informative educational debate becomes a war of slogans, where the two camps exchange insults, brandish their research papers and generally condemn their opponents as, at best, misguided and, at worst, downright evil. Caught in the middle, some school systems have found a way out by allowing both groups to have their own schools under the public umbrella. Appealing to the principle of parent choice, school boards in some cities have created both "back-to-the-basics" schools and "alternative" schools, with parents free to choose where they send their children.

Direct instruction has a place in teaching, especially when students have to master some basic content. There are certainly times when teachers must teach to the whole class, to give specific instructions, to take students step-by-step through some task, all the while giving them lots of drills and exercises so that they put into practice what they are being taught. Properly done, whole-class teaching can raise questions, provoke thinking and encourage students to explore problems. In the examples of the Greek city-state and castles, classes were not broken down into groups, and the teacher controlled the pace and direction of the lessons, but in ways that required students, not so much to answer pre-set questions, but to explore open-ended problems. There is also a place for group work, for projects, for debates and experiments, for assignments that call on students to think and explore for themselves. Some topics are best taught one way, and some the other. Some students learn better one way, some the other, and most benefit from both. Any competent teacher will use both as appropriate. In the end, what matters is not so much the choice of teaching methods, but the way the methods are used and the spirit with which they are given.

REFERENCES

1. William Peters. *A Class Divided: Then and Now*. New Haven: Yale University Press, 1987.

2. Herbert Kohl. *Growing Minds: On Becoming a Teacher*. New York: Harper, 1984, p. 9.

3. *For the Love of Learning: Report of the Royal Commission on Learning*. Toronto: Queen's Printer, 1994, VOL 1, pp. 78-9.

4. Jerome S. Bruner. *The Relevance of Education*. New York: Norton, 1971, p. 72.

5. A.B. Hodgetts. *What Culture? What Heritage?* Toronto: Ontario Institute for Studies in Education, 1968, p. 56.

CHAPTER SEVEN

Are Good Teachers Born or Made?

HOW SHOULD TEACHERS BE TRAINED?

ONCE WE HAVE DECIDED what we mean by good teaching, the next question is: How do we get it? Some people say that we must trust to luck. Good teachers are born, not made. Just as we cannot make a Picasso or a Wayne Gretzky, a Mozart or an Oscar Peterson, so we cannot make a good teacher. All we can do is sit back in admiration when we see one in action.

It is true that some people are born teachers but, like talented artists and athletes, even they benefit from training. And we obviously cannot put a born teacher in every classroom. There are simply not enough of them to go around. In the 1920s H.G. Wells said that the way to solve this problem was to make the world's best teachers available in all classrooms through film and radio. Today we are told that the computer is the answer. But even if this turns out to be correct, which seems unlikely, we will still need teachers, and if they are not born, they will have to be made. Any attempt to improve schools must pay serious attention to teacher training.

Systematic teacher training only began in the nineteenth century. Before then anyone could set up shop as a teacher, though often a certificate of good character was needed from the church or the local authorities. Teacher training only became a concern when governments made public schooling a responsibility of the state. Since public schools were set up to teach the official curriculum, using the officially authorized textbooks, it was important to ensure that teachers were qualified to do what they were supposed to do and that they did it. Teachers had to know what the curriculum was, how to teach it to the required standard and how to run a classroom. This is why the nineteenth century saw the creation of teachers' colleges, or normal schools, so called because they established a norm, a standard that teachers were expected to maintain.

Normal schools took students, who were primarily young women, straight from high school for a year or two and taught them the content of the subjects they would be expected to teach, together with some teaching techniques and a sprinkling of theory and philosophy. Normal school graduates for the most part went on to teach in the elementary grades, generally up to grade eight or so. Anyone who wished to teach at the high school level was expected to have a university degree, and only a few such people took normal school training. Some of them took a one-year teacher-preparation program that universities ran especially for this purpose, but many went straight into teaching with no training at all.

This division between normal school and university graduates was also a division between elementary and high school teachers, and in many ways a division between women and men teachers. It created a split in the teaching profession. University graduates were paid more than normal school graduates. They saw themselves as having higher status. The majority were men and as such were paid more than women. The two groups often had different career expectations and different priorities. In some provinces, notably Ontario, they formed different professional organizations.

By the 1960s this kind of division had begun to weaken. More teachers were getting university degrees, often through part-time study while they were working. Above all, in the educational optimism of the 1960s it was generally believed that two or three years of normal school were no longer enough for teaching at any grade level. Rather, all teachers should have degrees and should benefit from the broad education that universities were thought to offer.

Today almost all teachers have a degree, and some have two or more, but problems remain. Teacher education programs are not practical enough for the schools, but are too practical for the universities. Their graduates complain that they contain too much philosophy and theory and not enough classroom training. On the other hand, universities sometimes regard their education departments as being too concerned with the practicalities of the classroom and not enough with the kinds of research that universities see as important.

This is not entirely the fault of faculties of education. University education programs contain only a small number of education courses. In a four-year program, only one year is devoted to the study of education, and some of that is spent practice-teaching in the schools, with the other three years devoted to study in arts, science or other subject matter. These non-education courses are rarely planned with the needs of future teachers in mind. Professors of arts and science subjects see themselves as teaching their subjects, not as training teachers. Since an important part of teaching is knowing one's subject well enough to be able to make it intelligible to often immature students, this creates a problem. It is one thing to know something about quadratic equations, the plays of Shakespeare, or the Riel Rebellion, but quite another to know how to convert this knowledge into something young students can understand and find interesting, and from which they can benefit. To do this successfully requires a deeper knowledge of a topic than the average student teacher gains from a once-over-lightly standard arts or science course.

Nor are the strictly education courses necessarily of any greater help to student teachers, who often complain that they are too far removed from the reality of the schools. For the most part, student teachers say their teaching practice in the schools is the most useful part of their training, followed by their teaching-methods courses. Even here there are problems. At their best, teaching-methods courses are intended to be ahead of what is happening in most classrooms. They are supposed to prepare student teachers to improve teaching, not simply to continue what is currently done. The problem is that student teachers do not have the experience, the power or the status to change the schools. As trainees in a school, who are only there for a limited period, they are guests in someone else's classroom, not masters of their own. They are in no position to change the world overnight, even if they are naïve or arrogant enough to think they could.

The deeper problem is that it is totally unrealistic to expect teacher education programs to prepare teachers thoroughly for what they face in the schools. A four- or even five-year program of university study, most of which is devoted to learning subject matter, and only one term of which is spent in the schools, can never prepare teachers to the level that is needed and expected. All other professions, such as law, engineering, medicine and accounting, recognize this reality and deal with it through programs of internship, articling or other forms of professional training. They see a university program as only a basic preparation, which has to be followed by a year or two of on-the-job training. The military works the same way, putting recruits first through a program of basic training and then through one or more advanced programs of specialized training for particular jobs, from combat infantry soldiers to air crew. Only in teaching have we assumed that university graduates, whose program includes a bare minimum of school experience, are fully prepared for their professional careers. There have been occasional programs of internship or apprenticeship for teachers, but they have all been abandoned after a year or two because of practical difficulties in operating them or because they were found to be too expensive.

Teacher training has been the subject of much attention in the 1990s, particularly in England and the United States, though to a lesser extent in Canada. Broadly speaking, there have been five major changes:

1. Teacher training institutions have begun to make their training programs more practical and less theoretical, largely by increasing the amount of time spent on direct consideration of school realities, such as classroom discipline, student evaluation, working with special-needs students and so on. In some programs in the United States, education courses have been cut back to make room for extra courses in subject matter.

2. Teacher training institutions have established much closer links with schools. In England, teacher training staff are required to spend regular periods teaching in the schools themselves; school teachers have been more involved in the training of student teachers; and schools have been much more involved in the design and delivery of teacher training programs.

3. Much more time has been allotted to school experience within teacher training programs. In the U.S., several states have begun school-based training programs that either eliminate or drastically cut back the involvement of university education faculties. In Ontario and Manitoba, one-year after-degree teacher training programs have been lengthened to two, but only on the condition that the extra year be spent learning on the job in schools.

4. There has been a move to accrediting teacher training programs in the same way that engineering and medical training are accredited. This involves creating a set of standards of performance, monitored by an independent group that has the power to approve or disapprove programs on the basis of regular inspections. In British Columbia the provincial government has created a College of Teachers to do something like this.

5. In the United States, though not in Canada, teachers have been required to write competency examinations testing their knowledge of subject matter and of education. The 1988 British Columbia Royal Commission on Education considered this, but rejected it on the grounds that Canadian teachers did not need it and that pencil-and-paper tests proved nothing about the quality of teaching.

Many of these changes make sense. It seems obvious that training programs will benefit if they are linked as closely as possible with schools and if student teachers are required to spend more time getting on-the-job experience under proper supervision. And there is a growing body of solid research on teaching that provides a more solid base for teacher training than has previously existed. At the same time, schools might not be the best homes for teacher training programs. They are not equipped for full-time teacher training and teachers are already overloaded. Nor do most teachers have the time or the access to good libraries to stay in touch with the continuing research that should form the basis of teacher training. Making training programs more practical might also make them more conservative, preparing student teachers for what exists, but telling them little about alternative ways of doing things. For this purpose, the university still provides the best base, provided it works closely with schools, does its job properly and concentrates on research and its application.

The biggest gap in all the new reforms in teacher training is their failure to do anything about teacher internship. No matter how good a training program is, a teacher's first permanent job has an enormous influence. This is when, for the first time, a teacher is in total control of his or her own classroom, and no longer a guest on someone else's turf. This freedom is limited, however, for new teachers have to prove themselves, and this usually means fitting into the way their school does things. Moreover, new teachers often get the worst timetable in the school, the most difficult classes and the greatest range of lesson preparations. As in many jobs, most new teachers have to begin at the bottom. The problem is that this happens when, as brand-new teachers, they have no experience to draw on, no files of previous lesson plans and materials to use and little time to think about what they really want to do. With little preparation time at their disposal, anxious to do well in the eyes of other teachers and preoccupied with organization and discipline, they spend their hours in a feverish race simply to keep ahead of their students. In the circumstances, it is amazing that any good teaching takes place at all, and certainly not surprising that so many new teachers fall back on conventional ways of doing things, teaching, not as they were trained to teach, but as they were taught themselves.

WHAT ABOUT THOSE IN-SERVICE DAYS?

WHATEVER IS DONE ABOUT the training of new teachers, the further training of teachers already in the schools is also important. Some people believe that it is *more* important, since at any given time new teachers will always be a minority in the profession and will never have the power and influence of their more experienced colleagues. At present, schools are allowed to spend up to ten or so days a year on non-teaching purposes. Some of these days are given over to teacher-parent meetings and routine administrative chores, and some of them are set aside for training purposes. They are the "in-service days" that are so well-known to parents.

No one denies the value of good in-service training, but few people are happy with much of what now takes place. Parents are inconvenienced when schools shut down and they have to make alternative arrangements for child care. For their part, teachers often do not find in-service days helpful. They often consist of a visiting speaker giving some kind of pep talk or describing some new development in education, but usually with no follow-up. At best, teachers learn something of general interest but do not have the chance to apply it to their own circumstances. Even when an in-service session focuses on a local school issue, the half-day or one-day format makes it difficult to do anything that has practical value. Some schools have dealt with this problem by building continuing professional development into their operation so that the in-service sessions become part of an ongoing program devoted to a problem of local concern, but this can be often difficult to do, especially when teachers have to take it on as an addition to an already heavy workload.

At the same time, teachers have to keep up with new developments. The most obvious example today is the impact of computers in the classroom, but there are many others: new ways of testing and evaluating students, new teaching methods, new curricula and so on. In addition, all schools have particular problems they wish to address, perhaps to do with discipline, reporting to parents, working with problem students, school rules or bullying. As in any profession, teachers need systematic and continuing professional development.

Many teachers seek it through university courses as they take graduate degrees in education or some other field, but these courses sometimes have limited relevance to what they do in their schools. As a result, some provinces are now reexamining their salary schedules for teachers. These schedules usually award extra pay for extra qualifications but without specifying what these qualifications should be. A physical education teacher who takes a master's degree in, say, economics or chemistry will get a raise in pay regardless of whether he or she uses what has been learned in teaching. The argument for this is that anything a teacher learns can be of use, either directly or indirectly, and that anything that furthers a teacher's general education should be supported. The argument against is that if tax dollars are to be spent on teachers' salaries, then the public has a right to expect that any money spent is spent on things that are directly useful in the classroom.

As far as the universities are concerned, the problem is that they cannot design programs to fit an individual teacher's particular circumstances. For example, if I am a teacher with a special interest in how to reach a certain group of at-risk students, I am not likely to find a university program that gives me just what I need. Indeed, with university cutbacks and the resulting elimination of courses and programs, I might never find what I need.

Some school districts are getting around this problem by contracting with universities to offer custom-made programs for designated groups of teachers that are worked out jointly to do a particular job. This has some obvious possibilities, though there is sometimes a certain tension between the professional-development priorities of teachers and the academic assumptions of universities.

Various provinces are now suggesting that there is a way around all such problems—change the certification of teachers. As things now stand, once teachers graduate from an approved training program and have done one or two years of successful teaching, they get a teaching certificate that is good for life. They can be dismissed only for good cause. Some provinces are considering changing this to a system of short-term certification, so that a teaching certificate is good for, say, only five years and can be renewed only on the completion of an approved upgrading program. This suggestion is unpopular with teachers' unions, which understandably see it as a threat to teachers' rights and insist it is something that has to be negotiated, not imposed by government. Nonetheless, supporters of the move see it as a way of ensuring, first, that teachers' salary increases are tied to training that will be directly useful in the classroom and, second, that in-service training and professional development will be more systematically organized. The danger is that the idea of useful training might be too narrowly defined, so that teachers are prevented from pursuing a more general education. It could well be, for example, that a good program in philosophy and history might be of more use to a teacher than a rigidly defined program of workshops and short courses in specific classroom problems. There is also a risk that any attempt to tie teachers' certification to a continuing upgrading program may result in teachers collecting a random grab-bag of credits for attending conferences, going to seminars, taking workshops and so forth, which are little more than busywork. It is impossible to tell whether limited-term certification is a good idea or not in the abstract. It has some obvious possibilities, but everything would depend on how it was implemented. Simply to convert teaching certificates from life to a limited term would in and of itself achieve nothing of significance.

Some researchers see a way around all these difficulties through rethinking what it means to be a teacher. An English educationist, Lawrence Stenhouse, suggested in the 1970s that we build into teaching the idea of teacher-as-researcher. This would involve reorganizing teacher training and professional development, and the evaluation of teachers, so that teachers are held responsible for conducting a personal program of continuing research. It would also involve reorganizing teachers' workloads so that they have time to pursue such research. And it would involve rethinking the nature of research. Teachers would not be expected to become white-coated laboratory workers, busily conducting high-powered experiments. Rather, they would pursue what is called "action research." This consists of taking immediate classroom problems, such as how to reach a particular student, how to reduce the amount of time wasted in a class or how to teach fractions and designing a personal program of investigation and exploration to solve them. It is in a sense the educational equivalent of those approaches in industry that encourage workers to solve specific problems in the workplace.

Regardless of how it is done, in-service training and professional development is now beginning to be seen as a priority. Those who think schools need to improve see it as an important instrument of change. Those who are happy with schools the way they are similarly value it as a way of helping teachers keep up-to-date and become more effective in their work. There are various approaches to improving its quality and, as so often is the case in education, there is no one magic solution. Since it affects teachers' working conditions, it has to be a matter of negotiation between teachers' unions and management. We are no longer living in the days when what we learned at the beginning of our careers can carry us right through our working lives. It has sometimes been said of teachers with thirty years of experience that in reality they had one year of experience repeated thirty times. Perhaps it was possible to teach that way in the past, but no longer.

TEACHERS' WORKING CONDITIONS AND THE QUALITY OF TEACHING

GOOD EDUCATION DEPENDS ON good teachers. This is such an obvious point that it should not be worth making, but policy-makers seem to assume that they can improve things by changing the system while ignoring what happens to teachers inside it. If the money that is now being poured into curriculum development, testing, record-keeping and other one-shot cures were to be spent instead on helping teachers teach, we would all be better off. And one way of helping teachers teach is to change their working conditions.

Across the country teachers report that they are expected to do more and more with less and less, as funding is cut back while demands on the schools increase. Almost every investigation of Canadian schooling in recent years has shown that schools are increasingly expected to deal with non-educational problems. About twenty percent of children live in poverty across Canada, though this national average hides the fact that the percentage is very much higher in the case of First Nations and inner-city children. Many others live dangerously close to the poverty line. In most families both parents have to work to make ends meet and, as is well-known, increasing numbers of children live in single-parent families. The result has been that teachers have had to take on work once done by parents. In addition, schools have been expected to take on a wide variety of non-educational tasks, from street-proofing to AIDS-awareness. In the circumstances, it is not surprising that teachers have cried, *Enough*! In the words of the 1994 Ontario Royal Commission on Learning, "Expectations of the school system have increased dramatically, without any clear identification of priorities or adequate professional development. Many teachers feel unable to carve out a degree of manageability in their work; the result is a siege mentality."[1]

A hundred years ago, teachers were seen largely as robots, whose job it was to stuff the official curriculum into students' heads. Since the curriculum was already planned, backed up by specially prepared textbooks, supervised by school inspectors and tested by officially prepared examinations, there was not much for teachers to do except deliver it. In reality teachers faced a huge range of problems, but in the official view teachers needed a minimum amount of training, usually only a year or two after high school, and no preparation time, since most of their work had been done for them. Teaching

was, of course, never this simple. Teaching in isolated one-room
rural schools, housing all grades, where often few people spoke English, starved of resources and companionship, teachers had to cope
as best they could. And many teachers quietly rebelled against their
conditions, strayed from the official curriculum and looked for ways
to make school more interesting to their classes. Nonetheless, the
official definition of their work remained unchanged. Though there
were many grand words about their importance as missionaries of
culture and civilization, teachers were treated as enforcers of the
curriculum.

Over the years, however, more and more was expected of them.
Governments could not resist using schools for all kinds of socially
useful purposes: medical inspections, vaccinations, health education,
cadet training, Junior Red Cross, citizenship, gardening, tree plant-
ing, driver training—these and many other tasks came thick and fast.
Even when they were not made part of the official curriculum, these
tasks still imposed extra demands on teachers. At the same time,
teaching itself became more complicated. Bit by bit, at least until
recently, teachers were encouraged to adapt the curriculum to their
particular students, to use teaching methods other than lecture and
seat-work drills and to make their classrooms more interesting places
for students. Today even more tasks have been added. Teachers are
now expected to mainstream special-needs students into their regular classes, often with minimal help and advice. They are expected to
teach new and improved curricula, usually with little or no in-service
training or support. They are expected to work closely with parents
by telephone and in person. They are expected to play a part in running the school, instead of leaving everything to the principal.

All these new demands make sense in their own terms. The
problem is that teachers' working conditions have remained largely
unchanged. It is true that most teachers now get some preparation
time, but it is nowhere near enough. In most provinces in recent
years teachers have bargained, and in a few cases even gone on strike,
for preparation time. On average they have won at most a half-hour
a day in the elementary grades and one class period a day in the high
schools. And even these times are being cut back. In one Winnipeg
school division, teachers are now allowed one preparation period
a day for half the year but none at all for the rest. In Ontario, the
provincial government in 1998 announced reductions in teachers'
preparation time while at the same time increasing class sizes.

Teaching is far more than standing up in front of a class of students and telling them something, but even a lecture needs careful preparation. A lecturer has to think carefully about what he or she wants to say, about how to organize the lecture around a few key points, about what details to include and what to omit, about how to keep the audience interested and alert, about how to introduce and wrap up the topic, and about a wide variety of other details. Few of us can stand up and deliver a lecture impromptu. We have to think carefully about what we want to say and how we want to say it. Other teaching methods take even more preparation. For example, to organize group work involves far more than simply forming students into groups and turning them loose. Materials have to be prepared, group assignments have to be planned, possible problems have to be anticipated. A film or a video, if it is to be more than a time-filler, has to be previewed and assessed for its teaching potential. What purpose will it serve? How will the teacher check that students understand it? What backup exercises and activities are needed? How will students be led to think about what they watch rather than simply absorbing—or ignoring—it?

So-called informal or child-centred teaching is in reality very formal indeed. If it is to be more than busywork, it needs a high degree of organization, but in a way that is often not obvious to a casual observer. It resembles a hockey game where we admire the skill and speed of the players, without ever thinking about the long hours of conditioning, coaching, training and game-planning that went into the final performance.

I once had a student teacher who was in danger of getting a failing report from his supervising school. I was told that the student's problem was that he was trying to teach like me. I was not sure whether or not I should take this personally until I understood the point. The student had learned from me, or from someone, a relaxed and informal approach to teaching that built on students' questions, moved from point to point in unpredictable ways and generally appeared casual and relaxed. He had not learned that such lessons always have to have a purpose, that teachers always need a clear map of the lesson in their heads, and that the apparent relaxation of a successful lesson is not some go-with-the-flow improvisation but, rather, the result of a careful plan and a deep familiarity with the subject matter of a lesson. To watch this kind of teaching is like listening to a jazz musician. What seems to an outsider to be random doodling is the result of endless hours of training and practice, of a deep knowledge of music and an ability to improvise on a theme without ever losing sight of its structure. In this sense, teaching is like an iceberg: only a small part of it is visible, but that part depends on everything that exists under the surface.

Good teaching requires careful preparation. At the university level, it is assumed that a one-hour class requires at least three hours of time: one for preparation, one for follow-up and one for actual delivery. There is nothing like this in schools. Every survey that has been done in recent years shows that teachers see time as their enemy. They consistently report there is simply not enough time to do all that is expected of them and that they would like to do.

The 1994 Ontario Royal Commission on Learning saw a solution to this problem in relieving teachers of their non-academic functions and handing them over to health workers, counsellors and others, but it is not easy to see how this might work. It calls for new forms of co-operation between schools and social agencies that are easier to talk about than make work, and it ignores the reality that in the real world of school students' non-academic problems cannot easily be separated from their academic work. More often than not, teachers are the people who are best placed to deal with students' problems, but to do so they need time.

One of the less well-known lessons of Japanese education, which is so often held up as a model for our schools, is that Japanese teachers spend noticeably less time with students than do teachers in Canada. Researchers report that Chinese and Japanese teachers are astonished when they learn that American teachers (like their Canadian counterparts), spend nearly all their time in the classroom. Chinese teachers reacted this way to a standard North American teacher's schedule: "How could any teacher be expected to do a good job when there is no time outside of class to prepare and correct lessons, work with individual children, consult with other teachers and attend to all the matters that arise in a typical day at school!" In Japan, teachers spend no more than sixty percent of their school time actually working with children.[2] The remaining forty percent is spent on preparation, marking and planning with colleagues.

In Canada (and the U.S.) the situation is very different. And until it changes, we are unlikely to see any marked improvement in our schools. We take it for granted that for every hour lawyers spend in court or meeting with clients, they will spend many more hours in research, consultation and preparation. When we watch an athlete or a musician perform, we know that countless hours of training and rehearsal lie behind the performance, and that this is part of the job. Only in teaching, it seems, do we expect people to spend all their working hours in public view. Unless and until we radically improve the working conditions of teachers, schools are unlikely to change, especially at a time when it seems that students are increasingly difficult to teach.

REFERENCES

1. *For the Love of Learning: Report of the Royal Commission on Learning.* Toronto: Queen's Printer, 1994: volume 111, p. 4.

2. Harold W. Stevenson and James W. Stigler. *The Learning Gap: Why Our Schools Are Failing and What We Can Learn from Japanese and Chinese Education.* New York: Summit Books, 1992, pp. 163-4.

CHAPTER EIGHT

Should Teachers Be More Accountable?

TEACHING, TESTING AND REPORTING

TESTING AND TEACHING GO together. Students quickly find out that learning means taking tests. One of their favourite questions to teachers is, Will this be on the test? No matter how much teachers emphasize learning for the sake of learning, they usually have to resign themselves to students' concern with tests. Indeed, they often turn this to their own use, telling students, This is important; it will be on the test. Parents similarly often judge their children's success by the marks they get on tests and other assignments. For teachers, tests serve three purposes: one, as a sign of how well students have learned something; two, as a sign that something needs to be taught again or explained more clearly; and, three, as a way of motivating all but the most unco-operative students to study.

Testing is only one way teachers evaluate students. Teachers are always seeking to figure out what is going on in their students' heads. They read faces, think about students' questions, interpret behaviour, check with colleagues—all in an attempt to find out how effectively they are teaching and how students are reacting to them. Teachers often come to know their students so well that they see testing as almost unnecessary, since most of the time they can predict more or less how their students will do. Nonetheless, testing remains an important part of teaching. If nothing else, it yields marks that look objective when set down in a record book or sent home on a report card. Some parents these days loudly object to so-called anecdotal or narrative report cards, which try to tell them in words what their children are studying and how well they are learning it, but are quite happy to be told that little Johnny has got 63% in mathematics or 58% in geography, without ever wondering just what that precise percentage actually means.

These days, in fact, testing—or assessment or evaluation, as it is often called—has attracted new support. Not long ago I heard a group of teachers complaining to a minister of education that his government's fascination with testing students would mean that their teaching would be limited to preparing their students for the tests. "What's wrong with that?" answered the minister. "They will be good tests and so there's nothing wrong with teaching to them." He said elsewhere that it would be a considerable improvement. Instead of teachers wasting their time wandering off in a thousand and one different directions, which is what he thought they were doing, they would now have a sense of direction and purpose. As a result, standards would rise, Canadian students would climb to the top of the international testing tables, and the Canadian economy would be safe.

The minister's position is shared by many of the people who are unhappy with Canadian schools. In their view, tests provide useful information for assessing the quality of schooling. Experts can specify what students ought to know or do, and test results will show whether or not they can do it, thus providing a measure of the effectiveness of schools. A school where most or all students pass the tests will, by definition, be effective. Better yet, if the test results can be published, as they now are in various parts of Canada, and if parents can be allowed to choose their children's schools, there will be a rush to get into the good schools and a rush away from the bad ones. Thus, competition will help improve the quality of schooling.

Even if this public competition is not allowed to take place, administrators will still know which schools are good and which are bad and act accordingly. As test scores are collected over the years, they will show whether the quality of schooling is improving or declining over time. Just as business cannot operate without sales figures, profit-and-loss statements and productivity indicators, so education needs its test scores. They alone can provide the information that policy-makers need. How well do Canadian students do in mathematics or any other subject? Should they do better? Where do they need to improve? Which schools are doing a good job and which are not? What accounts for good test scores and what does this tell us about how we should teach? All such questions can be answered by a reliable system of testing—or so we are told.

Tests will also force teachers to stick to the curriculum, especially once they know that their performance will be judged according to how well or badly their students do on the tests. If the tests are well designed, they will inevitably improve the overall quality of schooling. They will also give parents and students a reliable and objective indicator of achievement. No more "Tom is doing as well as can be expected" or "Dorothy is performing below expectations," or wondering just what a B or a C+ means. Now there will be a mark, easily understood and objectively accurate.

These arguments have led provincial governments in the past few years to return to some type of provincial examinations. No province has restored the old one hundred percent sudden-death approach of external examinations in all subjects. Instead, they specify certain grade levels, often only certain subjects, notably mathematics and literacy, with other subjects being tested in rotation; and they include a percentage of school marks, ranging from seventy percent in the lower grades to fifty percent in the higher, in students' final marks. In Ontario and Manitoba these provincial tests begin as early as grade three and are timed for what are seen as important breaks in students' school life, usually grades three, six, nine and twelve.

This activity at the provincial level has resulted in schools and school districts taking testing more seriously at the local level. Most schools now have school-wide examinations of some sort, and an increasing number of school districts also have district-wide examinations in some subjects at various grade levels.

There is also a growing move to some kind of national testing across provinces, especially in mathematics, language and science, which are seen as the foundations of economic prosperity. The Council of Ministers of Education operates a School Achievement Indicators Program, which tests 13- and 16-year-old students' literacy and mathematics skills, and is exploring the possibility of testing other subjects. These tests, however, will not be taken by all students, but only by small samples. They are intended to find out whether students know more or less than expected and to help provincial departments of education decide on future curriculum policies. In addition, some provinces participate in international tests, especially in mathematics and science.

Teachers increasingly live in an environment of testing. They are being told to test more themselves and, whether they like it or not, find themselves having to prepare students for more and more compulsory tests, which they have no voice in making. Tests seem on the way to becoming the tail that wags the new educational dog. But, say the test-makers, we have nothing to lose and everything to gain, since the tests will be good tests and will work to everyone's benefit.

THE DEBATE OVER TESTING

MANY TEACHERS, HOWEVER, ARE unconvinced. In general terms they have four objections. First, they fear that more testing will limit their ability to teach. Increasingly they will have to teach to the test, and will not be able to adapt the curriculum to their students. They do not believe the testers' assurances that the tests will be good tests, which will challenge and motivate students. In the teachers' view, any test that is the same for all students at a given level must by definition ignore individual differences. Moreover, they insist, there is far more to education than what is measured on tests. But the new enthusiasm for testing ignores this.

Second, say the teachers, test scores do not accurately reflect what teachers do in the classroom, and certainly should not be used to measure teachers' effectiveness. It is a fact of life, for example, that students from middle-class, professional homes often do better at school than students from less privileged backgrounds. This happens, not because such students are brighter or their teachers better, but because they bring to school many advantages other students do not enjoy. To compare the test scores of, say, a culturally mixed inner-city school, wrestling with all the social problems its students face, with those of middle-class suburban schools seems grossly unfair.

Third, teachers fear that the emphasis on testing will hurt students rather than help them. There will always be students who cannot pass the tests and who therefore will be held back grade after grade, until they are shunted into low-track programs or simply give up on school in despair. Schools will become, even more than they are already, places where some students make it but others do not.

The social costs of this kind of segregation, say many teachers, will be seen in long-term unemployability, higher crime rates and antisocial behaviour that will far outweigh any hoped-for improvements in the academic quality of schooling.

Fourth, many teachers believe that the testers are promising far more than they can ever deliver. Everything in the history of education suggests that simply designing a new program or a new testing system will have very little impact on what actually happens in class-rooms, except perhaps to make life more difficult for teachers. In any case, the most serious problems facing the schools have their roots in the lives of students outside the school and so are largely outside the control of teachers.

Whether teachers are right or wrong, it is certainly true that large-scale, system-wide testing will never, on its own, improve the quality of education. At best, it will leave it unchanged. It could make it worse. Back in the days of provincial examinations, there were plenty of complaints about the poor quality of education. In 1950, university professors complained bitterly about what they saw as the low standard of high school graduates. The head of the English department at Queen's University estimated that a quarter of university students could not write acceptable English, even though they had passed grade twelve provincial examinations. In 1968 a national survey of Canadian-history teaching reported that the great majority of lessons were poorly taught, that students were not chal-lenged, that standards were unacceptably low, and that virtually no learning was taking place in history classrooms. It blamed this state of affairs on the conditions of the previous thirty years, thus push-ing back its criticisms into the 1930s. These complaints, and many more could be listed, came in the days when only a minority of stu-dents went to high school, when curricula were tightly policed, and there were external examinations. System-wide testing did not work then. There is no reason to assume it will work now.

This is why some schools are now experimenting with alterna-tive ways of evaluating students. They do not believe that any one-shot test or final examination, no matter how good, can ever give a fair picture of what students have learned. They also argue that tra-ditional testing does not reflect in any way the kinds of skills and habits that students need in real life. They want to evaluate students' ability to to meet "real-life" conditions. They speak of "authentic" assessment or achievement, which they see as a way of evaluating how students "frame problems, find information, evaluate alternatives, create ideas and products, and invent new answers to messy dilemmas."[1]

This approach to evaluation does not impose some kind of final examination at the end of a program, but rather arises from the work that students do during their programs of study. Usually it takes the form of an "exhibition" and a "portfolio." An exhibition is an end-of-course activity in which students display, explain and defend to a select group of judges, usually made up of teachers, parents, fellow students and people from the community, a long-term project on which they have been working, and which shows their skills and knowledge. It is an academic version of the kind of task apprentices once had to perform to demonstrate their mastery of their trade. Moreover, it does not stand alone but is accompanied by a "portfolio" of work that shows what a student has done in various subject areas. Portfolios contain essays, reports, tape and video recordings— and anything that shows what students can actually do and how they have progressed over a period of time. Portfolios are not simply random collections of work. They have to meet certain criteria and standards that parents, employers and other people from outside the school have a hand in establishing. Supporters of this portfolio approach say that one of its greatest benefits is the way it brings together teachers, parents, students, employers, universities and others to specify acceptable objectives and levels of performance.

This kind of evaluation is complicated, time-consuming and expensive, though often not as expensive as standard province-wide tests, which typically cost hundreds of thousands of dollars per subject to set and mark. But it possesses certain advantages. It allows for and even requires teachers and students to work together to meet specified criteria or objectives. Its results are visible, public and relevant to life after school, whether in the workplace or in further education. It allows employers to see firsthand just what students can do, which is why some employers are taking a serious interest in it. Rather than being imposed on a school from the outside, it arises directly from the work students do, while also shaping that work as students and teachers co-operate to meet specified levels of performance. And it combines the flexibility teachers and students need with the accountability society expects and demands.

ACCOUNTABILITY

THE PUSH FOR MORE testing is closely connected with the demand that schools should be more "accountable." This is an old problem. In the early days of schooling, schools were small and very much part of their community, and parents could easily find out what teachers were doing. Beyond this, examination results provided some measure of public accountability. Whatever went on inside the school walls, parents knew whether or not their children were passing their examinations. And since examinations influenced what schools did, report cards provided concrete marks for each subject, and often a school-average mark and a student's placement in class, so that parents could get some idea of where their children stood. Teachers knew that those solid numbers, such as 65% in mathematics and 70% in history, were in reality not nearly as solid as they seemed, but at least they provided some apparently understandable information.

By the 1970s they began to disappear. Provincial examinations were ended. Marks and letter grades were replaced by written comments. Students' placement in class was no longer publicized. Schools began to operate in ways that were no longer familiar to parents from their own schooldays. As a result a gap opened up between schools and parents, except in those cases where parents made a deliberate effort to stay in contact with schools or where schools made working with parents a major priority.

This gap became a major cause of concern in the 1980s, when parents began to realize that education could make a crucial difference to their children's futures. High school, they were told, was no longer enough. In the future, good jobs would require university training. Not surprisingly, anxious parents cast a sharp eye on their children's schools. Worried about what the future held for their children, and in some cases bothered by unwelcome changes in the larger society, they were already half inclined to look for the worst.

They sometimes found it. It was quickly obvious that standards varied widely among, and sometimes within, schools. More troubling, it was not always easy to tell just what the standards were supposed to be. Schools spoke about continuous progress, the importance of judging children as individuals or helping them reach their potential. Such answers made sense in terms of certain kinds of educational theory, but to parents they sometimes seemed to be a waffling "edu-speak" that served only to miss the point.

When parents turned to report cards, they found themselves no further ahead. Often, schools had abandoned marks, especially in the elementary grades, and replaced them with descriptive comments. When it worked, the change had much to recommend it. A mark, despite its black-and-white certainty, really says very little about what students can actually do. A well-written descriptive account of a student's performance, on the other hand, can say a great deal. Unfortunately many such accounts did not do this. In the first place, even the most gifted teacher can find it difficult to write thirty or more good reports in limited time, usually after completing a crowded and busy day, which is why schools often turned to computerized comments. In the second place, not all teachers were as skilled as they might have been in figuring out just what little Johnny could and could not do, or deciding just what little Janet's strengths and weaknesses were, and then explaining them in clear and straightforward English to parents who were not familiar with the specialized language of education.

Nor were teachers always willing to call a spade a spade. Teachers by and large are well-meaning people who want to think the best of their students. They are well aware of the dangers of labeling people and do not wish to upset parents. Unfortunately parents may not be clued in to the real meaning of what a teacher is trying to say. When teachers say that Annie is working hard and will improve with effort, they really mean that she is in trouble and likely to find the work too difficult. Annie's parents, however, read the comment literally and assume that as long as Annie keeps working, things will be fine. Researchers report that many teachers emphasize effort over achievement, especially in the case of students who are judged to be non-academic. Such teachers reward students who try their best, regardless of how well they actually do. Or rather, doing well is defined as doing one's best, whether or nor one reaches the prescribed standard. One teacher explained his approach to evaluating students this way: "So you tend to judge kids on how they perform in class in relation to other kids. But I try to do it on the progress of the child. What progress is he or she making? Are their writing techniques getting better? That kind of thing. So a B to one child would mean a completely different thing to a B for another child."[2] In many cases, however, parents, and certainly employers, want to know just what a B means in terms of a general standard.

Parents have to take some responsibility here, but to say this does not get rid of the problem. Not all parents visit schools, and in these days of working parents and single parents, often cannot even if they want to. They want to know just what the schools are trying to achieve and how they will measure whether or not they have achieved it. In other words, they want clear standards of performance and some way of ensuring accountability. In 1998 there was a minor controversy in Manitoba about provincial testing of grade three students. A small number of parents boycotted the test, on the grounds that grade three children were too young and that the test would not prove anything anyway. The majority of parents, however, supported the test as a way of finding out how well their children's schools were doing.

It is not difficult to see why this demand for accountability and standards can make teachers nervous. They are to be held responsible for the success or failure of students, regardless of circumstances. A teacher who has a problem class, or one where many students find English difficult, will be judged in just the same way as a teacher who faces nothing but straight-A students. A teacher, after all, can teach her heart out but still not manage to reach all her students. Moreover, as teachers justifiably see it, the odds are stacked against them. Class sizes are too large, preparation and follow-up time is largely non-existent, curricula are locked into year-long grade-by-grade sequences, and more and more duties are thrust upon them— but at the same time they are expected to make sure all students pass their examinations and they are held responsible when they do not. In the 1860s, England introduced a system of "payment by results" in which teachers' salaries were in part decided according to the test results of their students. No one has yet suggested this in Canada, but teachers can be forgiven for wondering if we might be heading in that direction.

Not all parents are up in arms over standards and accountability. Surveys consistently show that most parents are satisfied with their children's schools, though at the same time they worry about the school system in general. The general feeling seems to be that the system as a whole is a mess, but fortunately my children's school is an exception. Some parents actively oppose the whole back-to-basics approach, favouring instead "alternative" or "flexible" approaches to learning, where grade levels are combined, curricula are adjusted to students' interests (or quietly thrown out the window altogether), and a good deal of freedom and space is allowed to both teachers and students. Most large school systems now include some kind of alternative or flexible learning option. But usually parents who are satisfied with the schools (or when they are not, nonetheless find it easy to work with teachers) are not likely to make any fuss. In education, as elsewhere, the squeaky wheel gets the grease, and dissatisfied parents attract attention beyond what their numbers warrant, especially at a time when the media, the universities, employers and policy-makers draw attention to what they see as the shortcomings of the schools. Accountability has become an issue that will not go away.

Nor should it. Parents have a right to know what the system hopes to do with their children. I once asked a junior-high science teacher what he planned to do with his students in grade seven and he told me that his main goal was to get them ready for grade eight. Teachers must have a better idea than this of what they want their students to achieve.

When I taught high school history, I knew what facts (dates, events, names and so on) I wanted my students to remember, what ideas I wanted them to understand, what theories I wanted them to examine and what skills I wanted them to master. Knowing this, I was able to identify which students seemed be having trouble and what kind of extra help they might need. I was similarly able to identify those students who could handle and would benefit from extra work. Above all, I was able to justify to myself and others just what I wanted students to know and do, and why. In deciding that this date was more important than that, or that this event justified taking time to study it, I was constantly forced to ask myself why I wanted students to learn it in the first place. History has been famously described as "one damned thing after another," and in school that is sometimes all it is, but if teachers ask themselves why they want to teach a certain topic in the first place, they can avoid this particular danger. Equally important, they can explain their thinking to their students, so that they also see the point of what they are expected to do. The research is clear: when students understand why they are required to do something, even if they do not agree with it, their learning improves.

When teachers know clearly what they want to accomplish with students, they can also explain it to colleagues and parents and indeed, to the community at large. Citizens have a right to know what their schools intend to teach and how they will know whether or not they have successfully taught it. More than any other political system, democracy depends on the qualities of its citizens, and these qualities are to a certain extent learned in school. Schools are too important not to be held accountable for achieving certain standards.

This accountability, however, is more than measuring test scores and changing the format of school report cards, as is happening in some provinces. To hold teachers responsible for their students' success on examinations, while at the same time denying them the freedom to adapt the curriculum and locking them into the existing grade structure of schooling, might be to have the worst of both worlds. This is why some schools are experimenting with alternative ways of evaluating students. It is also why many schools are making a special effort to keep parents informed of what they are doing. It is now an expected part of a teacher's workload to telephone and even visit parents at regular intervals to tell them of their children's progress and to ask for their co-operation—and not just when problems arise, but as a matter of routine for all students. In addition, schools are increasingly establishing parent councils that have real powers, including hiring teachers and deciding school policies. This kind of two-way contact between parents and schools is likely to do more for standards and accountability than any amount of tinkering with the system.

Though no one has so far suggested it, perhaps the most effective way to combine the freedom teachers need with the standards the community has a right to expect is to reinvent school inspectors. Other countries make good use of them, but we simply eliminated them in the 1970s. At their best, school inspectors were far more than ministry of education enforcers. More often than not, they took the side of teachers against the ministry demands. They brought advice, support and help to teachers, especially in isolated rural areas. Competent school inspectors can monitor the standards that society expects to be maintained, while at the same time identifying those teachers who need support in meeting them. Such, at least, was my experience with inspectors in the 1960s. And they would cost no more, and likely considerably less, than the complicated and expensive apparatus of testing now being put in place.

REFERENCES

1. Linda Darling-Hammond. *Authentic Assessment in Action*. New York: Teachers' College Press, 1995, p. 5.

2. Alan J. C. King & M. J. Peart. *Teachers in Canada: Their Work and Quality of Life*. Ottawa: Canadian Teachers' Federation, 1992, p. 80.

Part 4

Students and Learning

CHAPTER NINE

The Lives of Students

WHAT IS A STUDENT?

THESE DAYS WE FACE two different definitions of what it means to be a student. One definition sees students as end-products. They enter school as raw material, and as they go through the process of schooling, they are formed and shaped until they emerge at the end of the process as finished products. This was the model that formed the foundation of the early public school system. Children entered the school to be shaped into citizens and workers. Once there, they were processed by their teachers, using the official curriculum and textbooks, with tests and examinations serving as quality control, until they became the sort of people the schools were intended to produce.

The other definition of what it means to be a student is more attractive to many teachers. It sees students not as raw material to be processed, but as individual boys and girls who need help to become men and women who can make the most of their lives. It sees education in terms of growth and development. Its model is not the factory, but the garden. Just as a gardener would never try to turn lettuce into a daffodil or a rose into a turnip, but would rather try to make them the best-developed plants they can become, so teachers are supposed to help children grow into competent men and women—not by forcing some curriculum on them but by appealing to their interests and providing the conditions for their full development. This is how, for example, the kindergarten got its name, which is German for "garden of children."

The first definition of what it means to be a student sees education as a journey with a set itinerary and a definite destination, which students either reach or not. It is something fixed and definite, like a marathon or the Tour de France, with clear benchmarks and signposts to indicate whether or not students are making progress along the prescribed route. It goes back to the original Latin meaning of "curriculum," which was race-course. The finishing-line is grade twelve graduation, defined as the achievement of certain set standards, and the itinerary is laid out by the curriculum, which requires that students do certain things in a certain order by certain times.

The second definition sees education as a journey without a fixed destination or even a fixed route. Students are expected to work as hard as they can to go as far as they can and, within limits, to choose whichever routes they wish to get there. There is no winning or losing in the usual sense. Failure is defined not as failing to reach some fixed point, but rather as not going as far as one could. Victory is defined as doing one's absolute best.

These are more than two abstract theories. They have very real consequences and are at the root of our current arguments about what schools should be doing and how well or badly they are doing it. The first says that schools should turn out the kinds of people society needs, with the skills and knowledge and values they will need as workers and citizens. The second says that that schools must help students make the best of their lives, that children are human beings in their own right and should not be seen as only workers and citizens.

As far as teachers are concerned, the first approach sees them as workers who turn out a specific product more or less according to specifications. Hence the language of objectives, outcomes and testing. The second approach sees teachers as professionals, like lawyers or doctors, who use their best judgment to help their clients, the students, as they see fit, provided they meet certain professional standards. These days most ministries of education in Canada take the first approach, while teachers understandably take the second, which is a large part of the explanation of the widespread distrust and suspicion that now exists between teachers and governments in many parts of Canada.

The conflict between these two approaches can be seen in every aspect of today's debates about schooling. Supporters of the first approach want report cards that contain marks, class placements, and so on; supporters of the second largely favour so-called narrative or anecdotal reports in which teachers use their own words to describe each student's progress and achievements. Employers and universities want to know just what a grade twelve diploma means; teachers say that their task is to help students progress as far as they can. Policy-makers favour external examinations and lots of testing; teachers say this will not tell them anything they do not already know. Policy-makers also want teachers to follow curricula more closely; teachers say that this will make it more difficult for them to motivate and interest their students. And throughout these disputes two different definitions of what it means to be a student are at work.

In the real world, these two approaches are not as cleanly separated as I have made them appear. Teachers and schools use both, so that the question becomes more a matter of emphasis than of choosing one and rejecting another. Nonetheless, there are times when a choice must be made, and this is increasingly the case in recent years. Most teachers prefer the second. It gives them more status, more freedom, more flexibility, and above all corresponds to the realities that face them daily in the classroom. Their choice, however, puts them out of step with the demands that are increasingly being made on the schools, which arise not so much from a vision of education as a fear of the future.

OUTSIDE THE CLASSROOM

MANY OF THE DIFFICULTIES teachers face in dealing with students have their origin outside the school. No doubt this has always been true, and teachers certainly faced enormous difficulties in the early days of schooling; but students today seem less and less able to leave their problems at the school door. In the words of an official of the Canadian Teachers' Federation, whose work keeps her in close touch with schools across the country, "Schools have never had to deal with so many students who couldn't care less, and who have so little reason to care more."[1]

Changes in the family, the lack of affordable day care, shifts in social values, economic insecurity—all have had an impact on the lives of many Canadian children. The promoters of downsizing, contracting out, cutbacks and all such measures designed to make the workplace meaner and leaner, shut their eyes to the impact of their actions on families. Many adults feel under stress these days as a result of fear about the security of their jobs, the need for retraining, and uncertainty about the future and the pace of change generally, and children have felt the effects of this stress. An American psychologist, David Elkind, has warned us against creating what he calls "the hurried child"—one who is so busy preparing for the challenges of the future, and whose parents have laid on so many organized activities, that there is no time to enjoy childhood in the present. In the words of Statistics Canada, "At the end of the twentieth century, the lives of children in Canada have never been so complex, the life chances of many of them never more uncertain."[2]

According to Statistics Canada, one in six children lives in a single-parent family, and most single parents are women living at or below the poverty line. The result is that parents can find it difficult to give young children the care and attention they need, especially when professional day care is either unavailable or unaffordable. It is estimated that one in five schoolchildren are "latchkey kids," coming home to an empty house at the end of the school day and having to fend for themselves. Just over half of working parents work in jobs that require irregular hours, usually in the evening or at nighttime, or on demand, so that they cannot guarantee being at home at the same time as their children or their spouse. About two-thirds of working parents report that between the demands of work and the responsibilities of parenting, tension is created.

All these developments have made teaching more difficult than it was, say, twenty years ago. There are still many committed and enthusiastic students in our schools, but there are also a growing number who find it difficult to accept the schools' values and standards. Their experience outside school has taught them to distrust authority. They see little value in the curriculum they have to follow. They challenge school routines. In many cases they are the victims of poverty, with all that means for schooling. As Ontario's Royal Commission on Learning put it:

> The essence of poverty is that it is a vicious circle: poor children are more likely to be of low birth weight; low birthweight children are more likely to have physical and developmental problems; children with physical and developmental problems

are more likely to have difficulties in school; even when there are no such problems, many poor families are so overwhelmed with the miseries that come from being poor they cannot provide a home environment that supports school learning; children who do poorly in school are likely to have employment problems.[3]

Apart from these social and economic problems, the role of the school has changed over the years. In the days before radio and television, the school served as students' window on the world. It was in school that students learned about other regions of Canada, about other countries, about the stars and other wonders. The natural curiosity of children, combined with their general lack of knowledge of anything outside their immediate surroundings, in some ways made teaching relatively easy. Much of what students learned was new to them and opened up worlds they did not know existed.

None of this is true any longer. Children probably get more information and general knowledge from radio and television, from film and magazines, from travel and conversation, than they do from schools. During their school years most children spend more hours watching television than they do in the classroom. When schools do teach new information, it can seem boring, since few teachers can compete with the glitzy messages of television and video. Teachers report that even the meaning of learning has changed. Learning now has to be entertaining. It has to be delivered with the pace and excitement of a music video.

Television has done more than change the way children learn. It has also introduced them to adult life and its concerns long before they are mature enough to deal with them. Even the most intimate aspects of adult life are now opened to children through easily accessible video and television programs. In a sense, there are no mysteries left. To a considerable extent, television has stripped parents, and adults generally, of much of their traditional authority over the young. With its dependence on advertising, it has also created a consumer culture that stresses the immediate acquisition of material goods. The result has been that children are surrounded by a rich variety of temptations they find difficult to resist, especially when their parents are preoccupied with their own concerns. According to two Ontario surveys in 1992 and 1993, one in five children between the ages of four and sixteen suffer from some kind of psychiatric disorder. A national survey of Canadian teenagers reported in 1985 that many teenagers believe they are not taken seriously and feel alienated from adults and adult institutions, including schools.

This kind of information is often used by social conservatives and religious fundamentalists to prove we are going to hell in a handbasket and to call for a return to simpler times, when women knew their place, children obeyed their parents, divorce was a disgrace and criminals were punished. However, we can recognize that our children face serious problems, even a crisis, according to some observers, without accepting these return-to-the-past solutions. As most experts put it, what is important is what families do and how well they do it, not what they look like, but it seems clear that an increasing number of families are in difficulty. In these circumstances, an adequately funded public system of day care and early-childhood education, as well as adequate support for working families with children, would probably be the most effective things we could do to improve the quality of Canadian education. The way it is now, however, we dump the problems into the lap of the schools and at the same time cut back on their resources, then criticize them for not doing enough to improve the academic standards of students.

Schools are doing what they can to cope with the problems students face. They run breakfast programs, teach non-violent conflict resolution, offer peer counselling, teach family life and sex education, organize antiracism and antisexism programs, campaign against drugs, reach out to parents and do a thousand other things they see as necessary, but that often take time and effort away from their academic priorities. This is why the 1994 Report of the Royal Commission on Learning in Ontario recommended a much closer and more systematic integration of schools with social service and community groups, so that the schools could concentrate on teaching and learning, leaving other agencies, working closely with schools, to deal with students' social and personal problems.

In many ways we are facing a social crisis that goes far beyond anything schools might do. Rather than face up to it, however, and see it in all its aspects, we find it easier to explain it as the failure of schools to do their job.

THE IMPORTANCE OF EARLY CHILDHOOD

SOME EXPERTS CLAIM THAT the first few years of life set the pattern for everything that follows, that in effect what we become as adults is decided in our first three years. Others believe that we can overcome our early influences, and that what happens to us and how we deal with it as we mature are just as influential as anything that happens in our early years. Whoever is right, the experts all agree that the first years of life have a powerful influence on the kind of people we become. These are the years when our image of ourselves and our attitude towards the world and other people begin to take shape.

We can learn that the world is a safe and interesting place and that we can control our own lives, or we can learn that the world is dangerous and unpredictable and that we cannot control what happens to us. We can learn to trust other people and treat them as we want to be treated ourselves, or we can learn that other people are cruel and nasty and we have to look after number one above all else. We can learn that we are capable and intelligent and can handle most things that face us, or we can learn that things are out of our control and we cannot do much about them. These things are not taught to us deliberately, through lessons in a classroom. We learn them from the way we are treated by our parents and others, young and old, by what we see happening around us, by what we see on television and movies and hear on the radio.

Besides what children learn in this unplanned and accidental way, increasing evidence suggests that their early years are not always as safe and supportive as they should be. We are all familiar with the horrific cases of child abuse and neglect that appear regularly in the news, and researchers estimate that these are only the tip of the iceberg. Experts estimate that as many as one in four Canadian girls and one in ten Canadian boys have suffered sexual abuse at some point in their lives. A 1991 poll reported that one in six Canadians said that they personally knew of "serious" instances of child abuse, and that more than a third did nothing about it. Even when not abused, too many children do not get the stimulation and support they need if they are to grow into healthy adults. They do not visit the zoo, library or museum; they don't have toys that stimulate their interest, books read to them, conversations that encourage them to think and question.

The result is that by the time many children reach grade one there is a danger their educational future has already been decided.

Unless schools make exceptional efforts to intervene, which may be beyond their resources and abilities, they can often do little more than play catch-up. Some years ago, for example, an American researcher, Raymond Rist, found that children's educational futures were decided even before they reached kindergarten. He found that some children responded to kindergarten much better than others. They spoke to the teacher freely, entered into the spirit of the classroom, brought things for show-and-tell sessions and so on. These children got more and more of their teacher's time and attention. By contrast, those students who were poorly dressed and sometimes unwashed, whose vocabulary was more limited, who interacted with the teacher less, received less of the teacher's attention.

None of this happened because the teacher was prejudiced or incompetent. Rather, she unconsciously gave more of her time and attention to those who responded to her and seemed ready and able to learn. The result was that by the end of kindergarten, some students were much better prepared for grade one than others. They liked school. They had more self-confidence and better social skills. They did better on tests of academic skills. Even before they began grade one, the grade one teacher already knew, from the reports of her kindergarten colleague, which students were likely to do well and which were not, which children it would be a pleasure to teach and which not. The predictable result was that by grades two and three, these differences had become "objective." They were entrenched in test scores and teacher reports. Some students were identified as bright, meaning good at schoolwork, and others as slow or dull.

The research on young children makes a strong case for putting more resources into the early years of childhood, beginning with parenting education, and including the right to high-quality and publicly supported day care. This is why the 1994 Report of Ontario's Royal Commission on Learning recommended a province-wide public day-care system beginning with three-year olds, along the lines of some European countries. Much of the educational debate of the 1990s has focussed on the high school, largely because of widespread concern about jobs and the economy, but this might well be putting the cart before the horse. The problems that face the high school often date back to things that happened in students' early years. By the time students reach high school, these problems can be difficult, if not impossible, to correct. Thus, it would seem to make sense to concentrate resources on the early years of childhood.

REFERENCES

1. Heather-Jane Robertson. *No More Teachers, No More Books: The Commercialization of Canada's Schools*. Toronto: McClelland & Stewart, 1998, p. 32.

2. Statistics Canada. *Growing Up in Canada: National Longitudinal Survey of Children and Youth*. Ottawa: 1996, p. 17.

3. *For the Love of Learning: Report of the Royal Commission on Learning*. Toronto: Queen's Printer, 1994, VOL. 1, p. 26.

CHAPTER TEN

Varieties of Students

STUDENTS WITH SPECIAL NEEDS

ONCE ALL CHILDREN WERE compelled to go to school, it quickly became obvious that something had to be done for those who, for whatever reason, could not handle the demands of the regular classroom. Children who were blind or deaf, for example, needed special arrangements. At one time, they were segregated into their own schools, partly because it was cheaper to put all such students into one building and partly because this made it easier to provide them with specially trained teachers who could give them the attention they deserved. There was a downside, however, since segregating such children in special schools meant that they were cut off from the wider society. This was especially true of students with mental handicaps, who had difficulty with regular schoolwork.

Within the past twenty years or so, there have been some important changes in the way schools approach all such students. Today, whenever possible, they are integrated into regular classes. The word most often used to describe this process is "mainstreaming," and and there are six major reasons it is seen as superior to the old custom of segregated classes:

1. The segregation of students can easily result in their being stereotyped as slow and different, with the result that they are not challenged. Rather than seeing them

as students who have *difficulties* in learning, people see them as students who cannot learn *at all*.

2. Segregating students into special schools cuts them off from the wider society and so fails to prepare them for life in the outside world.

3. Segregating students into special schools can create very low expectations of what they can do. Labelled as 'special' or 'disabled' or worse, they are treated as people who can do only the most routine things, if even that, and thus whatever potential talents they have may never be developed.

4. When segregated classes exist, students are too easily labelled as needing special help. For example, children with impaired hearing or vision were sometimes wrongly labelled as slow or handicapped, when their only problem was that they could not see or hear what was going on in the classroom. Or students were labelled as mentally slow when their only problem was one of attitude, not of ability.

5. Segregating students into special classes makes it too easy to lower expectations and avoid looking for more appropriate ways to teach them the regular curriculum.

6. Segregating students is a denial of their human rights, for whatever their level of ability, they are human beings and citizens and entitled to the rights of citizenship.

These are powerful arguments, but if mainstreaming is to be effective, it requires extra teaching staff in the classroom, often on a one-on-one basis in the case of children with severe difficulties. It means that classroom teachers need more time away from teaching to plan for the extra work and to supervise the required extra teaching staff and resource people. It also means that all teachers need training in how to work with students with special needs.

Few teachers have been this lucky. Their classes have been

mainstreamed, but except for the provision of teacher aides to help with students with severe difficulties, nothing else has changed. Preparation time has been cut back, little special training has been provided, and teachers find themselves with less time to spend on those students who are not labelled as having special needs and who make up the majority of the class. In the circumstances, and despite some notable successes, it is not surprising that many teachers see mainstreaming as a good idea that has not been given a chance to work as it should, and that has only made their work more difficult.

Despite the existence of mainstreaming, special-education classes still exist. A growing number of students these days are identified as having learning disabilities, ranging from dyslexia to attention deficit disorder, or as suffering from emotional or personality disorders that interfere with their ability to learn. More and more students seem to be fitted with some kind of ILP—individualized learning program—which calls for regular visits to counsellors, sessions with special-education teachers for remedial work or exercises, and a whole battery of tests and reports to ensure that whatever is thought to be wrong is being corrected.

All this activity is well-intentioned, but it has become too easy to label students just because they do not fit in. The danger of having psychologists, therapists and other experts on tap is that teachers are tempted to turn to them when faced with a problem student, rather than working out a solution for themselves.

Years ago, one of my own children turned against school when he was in grade five. A happy and successful student, he suddenly developed a severe dislike for school, to the point of throwing up at the very idea of going to school. After a few days my wife and I went to see the principal, whose only suggestion was that we should call in the school psychologist. I did not believe the problem was that serious. Instead I examined what was happening in the school.

The problem soon became clear. My son was being forced to take part in a school play. He was supposed to perform in a Japanese fisherman's dance, which made absolutely no sense to him, since he was convinced that Japanese fishermen did their jobs and lived their lives, but did not perform a ritual dance to celebrate a good catch. His teacher, however, insisted that her students had to do it. My son's response was not to protest or argue, but to bottle up his feelings until he became ill. Once the problem was uncovered, it took only a few minutes to work out with the school an alternative role for him, and life quickly returned to normal. If I had not worked in the school system and kept the psychologists and child-guidance experts at arm's length, who knows what might have happened? Unfortunately such experiences are more frequent than they should be in schools, with the result that too many children are officially labelled as "learning disabled" or "emotionally disturbed" and therefore in need of special education.

Special education also includes the education of students who are thought to be gifted or talented, and in recent years such students have attracted increasing attention. Schools have always tried to offer some kind of accelerated education for students who are considered especially bright. In the elementary school, this usually takes the form of pulling students who have been identified as gifted out of their regular classes for enrichment sessions, where they receive a more demanding level of program and teaching. In the high school, special curricula have been introduced, most notably the international baccalaureate and advanced placement programs, which offer a higher level of work than regular courses.

The main problem with all such programs is that by singling out a particular group of students as gifted, it is implied that all other students are not. The result is that so-called average students can get dumbed-down courses and a low level of teaching, since this is thought to be all they can handle. In fact, however, when one looks at the kinds of teaching recommended for gifted students, it does not seem to be beyond the capacity of those who are thought not to be gifted. Indeed, if it were offered to them they might well respond positively and prove to be more gifted than they appear. Providing special programs for gifted students also raises a question to which there can obviously be no definitive answer: When resources are limited, should the schools be devoting them to the education of those who will succeed anyway or to those at the other end of the scale who need all the help they can get?

MOSAIC OR MELTING POT?

Schools today, especially in the cities, find themselves dealing with students from a wide variety of backgrounds. It is not unusual to find classes where the majority of students speak neither English nor French as their first language, and where they share no one language in common. In one sense, this is nothing new. From the beginning, Canadian schools, at least in Ontario and the West, found themselves teaching a wide variety of immigrant children, speaking many languages and knowing little or nothing about their new country and its customs. Indeed, their task was to take such children and turn them into "good Canadians," speaking English (or occasionally French), obeying the law and following Canadian ways, while also retaining some of their own customs in their private lives. In this way, Canada prided itself on forming a "mosaic," in which unity and diversity are combined, unlike the "melting pot" of the United States.

Since the early 1970s, Canada has been officially multicultural and schools have encouraged more diversity than ever before. Besides French, English and aboriginal languages, many schools now offer heritage-language programs, while also including multi-cultural elements in such subjects as art, music, literature and history. They have downplayed their traditional Christian emphasis (as in the case of Christmas) in order to make way for festivals and beliefs from other religions. They have tried to work with parents whose values conflict with school policies, as in the case of coeduca-tional physical education or the teaching of certain novels and plays. In short, the schools reflect the overall multicultural makeup of Canada as it has evolved over the past thirty or so years.

This presents schools with particular problems. The curricu-lum, especially in subjects such as literature, history, music and art, has traditionally emphasized Canada's debt to western civilization, from ancient Greece and Rome through centuries of European influence. How then should schools respond to claims that this shows an unacceptably "Eurocentric" bias and even downright racism? It is relatively easy to put more First Nations, African-Canadian or other content into the curriculum, but how should schools respond to demands for curricula and even whole schools based on one particular culture? If Roman Catholics have a consti-tutional right to their own publicly funded schools, why should not other religious groups?

Some recent commentators have suggested that there is a risk multiculturalism can be carried too far, with the result that the things Canadians hold in common are swamped by all the things that make us different. The problem for the schools is how to com-bine a sense of Canadianism, of national identity and unity, with a respect for ethnic and cultural diversity. This question has no easy or single answer, and perhaps the most the schools can do is ensure that they teach students to think about it. It is of far more than philosophical interest for teachers, for they face its concrete application every day of their working lives.

BOYS, GIRLS AND GENDER

IT IS WELL-KNOWN THAT women are not on an equal footing with men in Canadian society. They earn less, hold fewer top-level jobs, are less likely to be elected to political office and still suffer from various forms of prejudice and discrimination. There are many reasons for this inequality and one of them can be found in the way schools have traditionally treated boys and girls. Reflecting the values of the wider society, schools for the most part have treated girls differently from boys, sometimes deliberately and sometimes without realizing it. For many years, schools saw boys as future breadwinners, and girls as future wives and mothers, and organized their programs accordingly. They steered boys to jobs in industry and to the professions, while girls were advised to become nurses, secretaries and teachers. The curriculum and textbooks reinforced these ideas and showed the world to be a world of and for men. Subjects such as history and literature described men's achievements and made it appear that women had little or nothing to do with the important questions of life. They either ignored women's experience or suggested it did not matter. Even in their day-to-day operation schools conveyed a message of male superiority. Until recently most school principals and superintendents were men, and women teachers were found mostly in the elementary grades, not high school. To sum up, a succession of reports concluded that schools were fundamentally sexist.

This has now begun to change. Most schools are now taking steps to ensure that girls and boys are treated equally. In terms of the curriculum, this means ensuring that women's experience is a part of all subjects wherever appropriate, especially in subjects such as history, social studies and literature. In science and mathematics, students are taught about the contributions of women. Girls are given special encouragement to take subjects they have traditionally avoided, such as mathematics and science, while both boys and girls now take home economics and industrial arts. Boys and girls increasingly share the same physical education classes. Teachers have also been given special training to avoid treating boys and girls differently. Traditionally boys have commanded far more of teachers' time and attention than have girls. They are more assertive, louder, more active, more likely to be discipline problems, and more inclined to answer teachers' questions, with the result that girls often find themselves pushed into the background. In addition, boys are inclined to show off, put girls down and sometimes engage in out-and-out sexual harassment.

Some schools are experimenting with all-girls' classes, especially in subjects such as science and mathematics. Only in this way, they say, can girls get a fair chance to develop, without being distracted or overshadowed by boys, especially in the early teenage years. This approach is supported by recent psychological research that suggests, even if it does not absolutely prove, that women and men have different ways of learning. According to this research, girls and women learn best when they are allowed to share with one another, to explore ideas and problems together, to look for links with what they already know, to pursue hunches and to make connections. The research does not say that this way of learning is unique to women or some kind of genetic endowment, but rather that it is something girls learn early in life and is too often ignored in schools. Some researchers believe that it is now possible to identify a way of teaching that suits girls better than boys, which will therefore make them more successful in school.

School staffs are also moving to become models of equality between men and women. For example, more women are being appointed to senior positions, while more men are teaching at the lower grade levels, which have been traditionally dominated by women. All school policies, whether concerning staff or students, are checked to see that they contribute to equality between the sexes. Schools are also doing what they can to ensure that boys and girls treat each other properly. Boys often treat girls unacceptably, ranging from name-calling to touching, especially in the teenage years when they are aware of their sexuality, but increasingly even when they are younger. In particular, they learn sexist ways of talking to and interacting with girls from television and video. Schools are increasingly on the lookout for sexual harassment, to correct it when it occurs and, where possible, create conditions that will prevent it from happening in the first place.

In short, schools are part of the struggle in the wider society to ensure equality between the sexes, both by acting as models of equality and by doing all they can to ensure that girls, as well as boys, are able to get the full benefits of education.

CHAPTER ELEVEN

How Students Learn

WHAT IS LEARNING?

AT ONE TIME WE THOUGHT of learning as listening to the teacher, doing assignments, practising skills, memorizing information and generally absorbing whatever messages were aimed at us. Learning was seen as a passive activity in which learners simply soaked up, like sponges, whatever was taught to them.

In reality, however, learning is much more complex. Some students learn more quickly and easily than others. Some have long attention spans; others do not. Some learn better from doing things with their hands rather than from reading. Some need pictures, diagrams, models and other concrete aids to help them. Students learn in different ways as they get older, indicating that there is a process of development in learning. And often students' answers show that what they have learned is different from what their teachers have taught them.

Learning is an active process in which learners try to make their own sense of what is taught them. They use their brains, not just their memories. Learning is not just remembering and repeating; it is understanding and interpreting. Learners' minds are not blank slates. They are full of memories, experiences and ways of thinking, which are used to understand and make sense of what is taught.

The question quickly becomes, just what goes on in students' heads when they learn something? A second question quickly follows: once we understand what goes on in their heads, what does it mean for the way we teach and organize curricula? The attempts to answer these questions have changed our idea of what it means to teach. They have also created something of a divide between teachers and parents. Some of the criticism that is directed at the schools these days arises from this conflict between two views of teaching. On the one side stand teachers, backed by psychologists and other researchers, who have largely accepted the theory of active learning. They speak of students as discoverers, inquirers, explorers, who learn best by discovering things for themselves. On the other side stand many parents, employers and others who hold to the older view of what it means to learn.

The first group argues that students will forget most of the factual information they are taught, so that what they need is not a well-filled memory but the ability to find information when they need it. In their view, students are not empty jugs, but computers. They need to be, not filled up, but programmed with the necessary skills of critical thinking, data gathering and problem-solving.

The second group is not so ready to dismiss factual knowledge and memory. They point out we still need a well-filled store of general knowledge to make sense of the world, to understand what is happening around us and to exercise our imagination. We cannot always be rushing off to find information when we need it. Rather, we need some basic knowledge of history and geography, of mathematics and science, of literature and the arts. If we have never been taught about, say, Leonardo da Vinci or Joan of Arc, Confucius or Cleopatra, if we don't know how electricity works or what influences the weather, we will never know how much we don't know, and our lives will be that much the poorer.

The argument is, in effect, between two views of learning. The first emphasizes "knowing how" and values skills. The second emphasizes "knowing that," and values factual knowledge. The problem is that, as is so often the case in education, the two views are frequently seen as mutually exclusive, with the skills people dismissing facts as unimportant, or at best as simply means to an end, and the facts people seeing skills as empty and without value. In reality, of course, both facts and skills are important. The trick is to find ways of doing justice to them both.

This is where the view of learning as an active process comes in. We know that even very young children are not simply empty bundles of sensation waiting for the world to act on them. As things happen to them, they try to explain them. They also try to influence the world around them, as they discover that their actions can often provoke certain responses. Crying might bring food or a cuddle. Teasing the cat might bring a scratch or a little lecture on how to treat animals. In either case, children realize that by doing something they can cause the world to react to them. And so, bit by bit, children collect experiences, ideas and facts, which they use as the foundation on which they build further explanations. By the time they reach their teens, they begin to think using logic and reason.

In other words, as children grow and mature and interact with others and their surroundings, they learn and think in increasingly complex ways. They begin by making sense of their world in ways that by adult standards are often completely illogical. Then they move to a stage where they can explain things, but only in concrete and limited ways. Finally they reach a stage where they are more or less comfortable with abstract ideas.

Perhaps the best illustration of this process of development is to be found in the work of E.A. Peel, a British psychologist. He presented students with problems that went like this:

> Only brave pilots are allowed to fly over high mountains. One day a plane was flying over some mountains and hit a cable railway, causing a cable car to crash to the ground. Several people were killed and others were injured. Was the pilot careful?

At the earliest stage of learning, children are fooled by the red herring in the opening statement and say that the pilot was careful because he (or she) was brave. Older children do not fall for this. They say that the pilot was obviously not careful because the plane hit the cable railway. No further explanation is needed. By their early to midteens students say they cannot tell whether the pilot was careful or not, because they need more information. What was the state of the weather? Did the plane suffer an engine failure? And so on. In other words, these students can think up a range of possibilities that go far beyond the information they are given and in effect turn the question upon itself.

Psychologists do not agree on just when or even why children move from one stage of thinking to another. Some believe that the most advanced stage only begins in the high school years. Others say it can begin much earlier, especially if teachers and parents encourage children to ask questions and to think for themselves. Some say that the growth in learning is the biological result of age and maturity, and teachers can only adjust to it. Others say that with thoughtful teaching children can learn in ways that might surprise us.

Whatever the answers to these questions, most psychologists and educationists agree that if children are to learn the most that they can, in the sense of both learning-that and learning-how, we must take into account how their minds work.

A NEW VIEW OF LEARNING

The technical word for this approach these days is "constructivism." It comes from the straightforward idea that when we learn, at any age, we are constructing meaning for ourselves. We do not simply soak up what others tell us. We test it against what we already know or think we know. We check it against our own experience. We put it in terms that make sense to us.

Constructivists see teaching as helping students arrive at their own explanations of things, which they can check against reality and continue to test, and by so doing stretch the limits of their thinking. They believe that old-fashioned chalk-and-talk teaching does little to or for students' minds. It substitutes information for thinking and limits students to learning what others think rather than learning to think for themselves. Obviously, this is not an either-or matter. No one thinks in a vacuum. We need knowledge and information if we are to have any thoughts at all, and certainly if we are to see whether or not our ideas make any sense. But for the constructivists, it can never be enough simply to learn what is already known. Knowledge must be used as a springboard from which students can arrive at, explore and test their own ideas.

Opponents of constructivism reply that most students are simply not ready for this, and that, even if they were, the first task is to learn what is already known, They must walk before they can fly. Children are not and cannot be philosophers or research scientists, and any attempt to make them so will be time wasted—time better spent on getting a solid grounding in the basics of the subjects that should be the basis of the curriculum, such as mathematics, history, geography and language.

Constructivists also see learning as a co-operative activity. In their view, we learn best by working with others in the exploration, analysis and solution of problems. Two heads are better than one, and a whole classroom of heads is better than two. Constructivists require students to work together, to learn from and with one another, to share their ideas, to challenge one another—hence the emphasis on group work in many classrooms today.

Opponents of constructivism do not oppose group work as such, but they do feel that there is far too much of it in today's classrooms, and that it is too often badly organized and without a sense of purpose. They also point out that it is more suitable for some classroom tasks than for others. If, for example, students have to learn some basic facts in history, some rules of grammar or some problem-solving techniques in mathematics, it is often best for the teacher to teach them directly to the whole class. They also point out that whole-class teaching can be done in a lively, student-centred, question-raising way.

Constructivists insist that group work has to be much more than an opportunity for social chitchat. Students have to be involved in working through a problem or a question that calls for genuine thought. As psychologist Jerome Bruner puts it, learning is best when it is "participatory, proactive, communal, collaborative, and given over to constructing meanings rather than receiving them."[1] The idea is not just to learn that Ottawa is the capital of Canada, but to examine why and how it came to be so, to consider whether other choices might have made more sense, and even to explore what is involved in the very idea of a capital city.

Critics see such activity as a time-wasting exercise in what-might-have-been, as involving children in work that is far beyond their capacity, and as taking up time that could otherwise be spent in learning useful knowledge. Constructivists reply that their approach is more in tune with what we know about how students think and learn, and is more likely to turn students into successful learners, who both like and know how to learn. They favour what has been called a "multidimensional" approach to teaching:

> Multidimensional classrooms provide a variety of learning tasks that require a broad range of skills. Students often cluster in small groups. They exchange ideas, work on separate but interrelated

tasks, and help each other learn. Teacher talk does not dominate, and neither do whole-class sessions of questions and answers. Teachers in these classes function more like orchestra conductors than lecturers. They get things started and keep them moving along. They provide information and point to resources, attend to the social skills children need for learning (asking one another questions; offering help; not putting others down), and co-ordinate a diverse but harmonious buzz of activity.[2]

Critics of constructivism see this picture of a classroom as so idealistic that it is out of touch with reality. In their view, constructivist teaching makes demands that most teachers cannot meet. It requires time for planning that they do not have. It requires a rich variety of resources that they cannot afford. It requires a breadth and depth of knowledge and skill that only the most exceptional teachers possess. And most fundamentally it deprives students of the expertise and knowledge that a teacher should have and be expected to pass on to students. They agree that a teacher can be compared to an orchestra leader, but they point out that orchestras follow a tightly scripted score, where everyone already possesses a high degree of skill and knowledge and understands where he or she is heading. The job of the school, they insist, is to pass on to students the wisdom of the ages, not to teach them to interpret the world anew, as though they were the very first people ever to do so.

Constructivists also argue that their approach is suited to all students, whereas the more traditional emphasis on memory and drill excludes many students who find it either uninteresting or difficult. Only a minority of students, according to constructivists, will willingly sit down and learn a list of dates in history or definitions in science, or read a Shakespeare play. Most students find such work either boring or pointless and either have to be forced or seduced into doing it. Hence teachers' never-ending concern with discipline and motivation. Constructivists say that their approach to teaching, by contrast, calls on students to use their minds, to think, to imagine, to do more than just memorize information, and that this is something that everyone likes to do. It makes schoolwork interesting to almost all students by linking it with their experience and showing them that it is something to be investigated and thought about, not just memorized. Rather than giving students answers to questions they never asked and in which they are not especially interested, it encourages them to frame their own questions and to search for answers. It also shows students that they can often do more than they realize. Given the right teaching, so-called slow students often prove to be not slow at all; their apparent slowness arising not from a lack of ability but from a failure to respond to conventional schoolwork. In short, constructivist teaching, say its supporters, shows most children to be more intelligent than they are often judged to be—and often think themselves to be. As a result their self-confidence improves and they are better prepared to go on learning.

MEASURING INTELLIGENCE

FOR MANY YEARS SCHOOLS operated on the assumption that intelligence was something fixed and measurable, like blue eyes or brown hair. They believed that every student had a fixed amount of intelligence, which could be reliably measured by tests and described in terms of a person's intelligence quotient, or IQ. The average IQ was fixed at 100, so that people who were below this level were seen as less intelligent than normal, and those above as more intelligent.

This approach to intelligence was initially welcomed by schools. It made it possible to sort students according to their IQ, and therefore according to their ability, which was assumed to be more or less the same thing. Teachers would no longer have to waste their time trying to teach something to students who were not bright enough to learn it, or teaching bright students something they already knew. For the first time, teaching would correspond to students' ability to learn. And thanks to IQ tests and intelligence experts, the whole process would be scientific. No longer would schools have to guess what to do with their students. Instead students could now be accurately assessed and sorted. This was especially important from the early 1900s onward, as high schools began to offer a wider variety of programs, university entrance, technical, commercial, vocational and the rest, and to wonder just which students belonged where. From now on, students could be matched to programs through measuring their intelligence.

Some European countries sort students at about age eleven into different kinds of schools, partly on the basis of intelligence and other tests. A small minority of students are sent to university-entrance schools. A slightly larger group are sent to technical schools. The great majority are given a basic, vocationally oriented education and turned out into the job market as early as possible. Canada never went to this extreme, but Canadian schools did use intelligence tests to sort students out into classes that were streamed by ability and into different kinds of programs. Even today, intelligence tests are one of the measures used to decide which students should be put into programs for the gifted and talented.

From the beginning intelligence tests have had their critics. Socialists, for example, have always been sceptical of them, believing that intelligence is a product of people's life experience, not of their heredity, and can be influenced by what schools do. In this view, the job of the school is not to adjust teaching to students' so-called level of intelligence, but to do everything it can to raise that level for all students. Socialists and others are struck by the way intelligence, as measured by intelligence tests, so neatly corresponds to differences in social class and race. Middle-class people, it seems, have higher IQ's than working-class people. Of course, said the defenders of intelligence testing, that is exactly why they are middle class: they are more intelligent. Others, however, are not convinced. Nor are they convinced that white people are more intelligent than black, or northern Europeans more intelligent than southern or eastern Europeans, all of which has been suggested by intelligence tests. The whole idea of intelligence seems to be too much of a rationalization of the status quo.

Some critics have accused the tests of being biased in favour of certain kinds of knowledge and experience, and so testing not raw intelligence, but the results of upbringing and family background. Other critics have gone further, seeing the root of the problem in the very idea of a fixed level of something called intelligence. They believed this even more when the intelligence experts proved unable to agree on a definition of just what intelligence is, with one sceptic concluding that intelligence is whatever is measured by intelligence tests.

In recent years schools have become much warier of intelligence tests and, to a lesser extent, of the whole idea of one uniform, fixed intelligence. In the 1950s, the psychologist J.P. Guilford broke it down into some eighty different abilities. More recently, Robert Sternberg, a Yale University psychologist, suggested that we all have three kinds of intelligence. One consists of our ability to analyse and work out problems; the second is the ability to think of new solutions to problems; the third is the ability to get through life's daily difficulties successfully. Most recently of all, Howard Gardner, a Harvard University psychologist, proposed that we all have at least seven intelligences. They are: linguistic, logical-mathematical, spatial (as in architecture) musical, physical (as in dance or sport), interpersonal (the ability to interact with other people) and intrapersonal (the ability to understand oneself).

The details of these theories do not matter here as much as their success in weakening older conceptions of intelligence. They open up the idea that we are all intelligent in various ways. They propose that no one form of intelligence is superior to another, and reject the idea that one can properly call some people more intelligent than others. This implies that what schools have traditionally emphasized, which is above all the ability to use language and numbers (the first two of Gardner's seven intelligences) and to think critically, are not and should not be the only priorities in schooling. It also implies that schools should design curricula to foster the development of all seven intelligences in all children, and indeed a few schools, though so far mostly in the United States, not in Canada, have set out to do precisely that. Even in Canada, however, Gardner's theory of multiple intelligences has struck a chord with teachers, who appreciate being able to reward students whose talents lie outside the linguistic and numeric aspects of conventional schooling, and it is increasingly common to see lesson plans and teaching units making specific reference to his work.

It is still too early to tell how all this will play out. There is a risk that the new views of intelligence will lead to a reduced emphasis on literacy, numeracy and other basic school priorities, as teachers seek to give equal priority to all seven intelligences. However, this need not be so. Gardner insists that none of the seven intelligences should be neglected. He also insists that some of the seven will be more useful in some cultures than in others, and in our culture linguistic and logical-mathematical intelligence are obviously extremely important. Perhaps the most important consequence of these new views of intelligence is that they help lay to rest the long-standing idea that some students are just naturally less intelligent than others and therefore there is nothing much schools can do for them. Long ago, before education was taken over by psychologists, teachers used to say (certainly mine did) that effort was more important in learning than intelligence, that, at least as far as schooling was concerned, anyone could succeed if they worked hard enough. The new views of intelligence might prove them right.

WHAT DO STUDENTS KNOW?

A CYNIC WOULD NO doubt answer this question by saying "Not much." In the past few years, surveys have shown that Canadian students know all too little Canadian history, generally scoring less than 50% on tests of the most basic knowledge. Employers and universities often complain that too many high school graduates cannot read or write at an acceptable level. Internationally, on tests of mathematics and science, Canadian students generally score in the middle of the pack, coming well behind students in Japan, Singapore, South Korea and some European countries. All this has led critics to condemn schools for their low standards and to call for a tougher approach to curriculum, examinations and teaching. Canadian students, it seems, do not know enough and need to learn more.

No one can be happy with the results of the various tests and surveys of the past few years, but there are some things that have to be borne in mind. Perhaps the most important is that there is nothing new in these findings. Universities have long complained about what they see as the low standards of the high schools. What they say today is no different from what they said in 1950 when presenting briefs to the Royal Commission on the Arts in Canada. To quote the head of the English Department at Queen's University:

> University instructors are continually faced with the problem of the student who cannot write his own language correctly. They do not expect distinction in writing or stylistic graces, but they feel that they have the right to demand at least mechanical correctness. At the university level a student ought to know what is a sentence and what is not a sentence; he ought to be able to apply the basic principles of punctuation without effort; he ought to have a reasonably varied vocabulary which he can use with accuracy. These are the minimum requirements that unfortunately a good many students do not meet.[3]

Ever since the 1920s we have bewailed our youngsters' ignorance of Canadian history. And no matter what we have done to change curricula and teaching methods, nothing much has changed over the years. The reasons are easy to understand. Knowledge of the past is not a high priority for most teenagers, and taking one or two history courses in school is not likely to change much of anything. This is especially so when what is taught in school is not reinforced outside the school. Canadian youngsters will learn in school that John A. Macdonald was the first prime minister of Canada, but they will rarely hear that fact repeated outside school. They listen to American music, watch American television and read American magazines, and so they rarely learn much about Canada's history in their everyday lives. Even in countries that are more patriotically exhibitionist than Canada, such as the United States, Britain or France, surveys show that their students know no more about their history than Canadians do of Canada's. If Americans can identify George Washington or Abraham Lincoln—and many know little more than the names—it is not because American schools do a better job of teaching history, but because Washington and Lincoln are icons in American culture, whose names appear again and again, from sitcoms to commercials, in ways that are not true of any Canadian figure, past or present.

Similarly, the international tests of science and mathematics have to be seen in context. The results are not especially flattering for Canada, but there are often only a few points separating Canadian students' performance from those of countries above them, which suggests that if only one or two questions had been different, the results might have been different also. And, as has been pointed out many times, how well or poorly students do on international tests depends to some degree on the extent to which a country's curriculum is consistent with the test that is set. It can happen, after all, that in any given country students will find themselves trying to answer questions on material that has not been taught them, either because it is not on their curriculum or because it comes in a later grade.

A country's performance on an international test will be influenced by the kinds of students taking the examination. In a country where all students stay in school until grade eleven or twelve, results will likely be lower than where only a small number of students stay on in school, since those who stay on will usually be more academically inclined and taking more advanced courses. In

other words, as has often been said, it is very important when looking at the comparative results of international tests to make sure that
all countries involved were facing similar conditions. It is equally
important to know just what questions were asked and to see how
they fit with the curriculum of the schools and therefore with what
students did in fact learn.

This does not mean that Canadian students do not need to
know more than they do now, both in terms of knowledge and
skills. They obviously do and always have done. But we will not
achieve this by turning the clock back to some golden age that never
existed. Things might not be what they used to be, but then they
never were.

REFERENCES

1. Jerome S. Bruner. *The Culture of Education*. Cambridge: Harvard University Press, 1996, p. 84.

2. Jeannie Oakes & Martin Lipton. *Making the Best of Schools*. New Haven: Yale University Press, 1990, p. 70.

3. *Royal Commission Studies: A Selection of Essays Prepared for the Royal Commission on National Development in the Arts, Letters and Sciences*. Ottawa: King's Printer, 1951, p. 18.

Part 5

Schools and
School Organization

CHAPTER TWELVE

Alternatives, Variety and Choice

SCHOOL CHOICE

HISTORICALLY CANADIAN STUDENTS HAVE not been able to choose schools. In rural areas there was usually only one school anyway. In towns and cities, children went to their neighbourhood school, no questions asked. No matter what the school, teachers were all supposed to follow the same curriculum. Students all wrote the same examinations, and inspectors and other supervisors made their rounds to see that everyone was doing what they were supposed to be doing. Schools inevitably took on different personalities, depending on the area they served, the character of their teachers and so forth, but their similarities were much greater than their differences.

In recent years this has begun to change. Parents want different things for their children. Psychologists have shown us that children learn in different ways. Students are no longer as willing as they once were to suffer in silence. We now give more importance to choice and difference in all walks of life. Not surprisingly, then, we no longer believe that schools should all be cut from the same cloth. Where numbers allow, school boards have begun to create schools that offer genuine alternatives to parents and students.

Some city school boards have begun to set up "magnet" schools, which are high schools with a particular curriculum focus, sometimes in music, drama and the arts, sometimes in specific technologies such as computers and so on. Some parents, and indeed some teachers, want, not so much choice of program content, but choice in the way programs are taught. Some favour a traditional back-to-the-basics approach, with students sitting in rows, working on their own rather than in groups, perhaps wearing school uniforms, with greater emphasis on drill and lecture in teaching. Others prefer a more student-centred approach, with lots of flexibility, combined grade levels, experimentation with curriculum and other innovations. Where they have enough schools, as in large towns and cities, school boards are increasingly moving to provide this kind of variety.

Even where they are not, they are more and more allowing students (or their parents) to choose which school to attend; students are no longer limited to their local neighbourhood school. Some provincial governments have taken this one step further by allowing students to attend their choice of school, regardless of school-board boundaries. This is one reason it is now commonplace to see schools, and especially high schools, advertising their achievements on billboards. When students and parents can choose their school, schools are forced to compete for their favour. A drop in attendance can mean a loss of reputation, a drop in funding and a loss of jobs for teachers. To prevent this, schools are increasingly forced to market themselves.

This kind of choice and variety exists within the public school system. It is an attempt to allow for difference while insisting on a minimum level of commonality, especially in the content of the curriculum. Canadians schools have long valued schools for their contribution to a sense of national identity and citizenship. From their beginnings, public schools have argued that by allowing, even requiring, children of different religions, languages, races and ethnic groups to play and work together, they make a valuable contribution to Canadian society. In the public school children learn to appreciate what they have in common as Canadian citizens. Thus, a real question exists: How far can the schools go in catering to choice and difference before they find themselves contributing, not to tolerance and unity, but to difference and distrust? Canada has long prided itself on being a mosaic rather an American-style melting pot, a society in which every group can retain its own identity while also forming part of a larger whole. In a mosaic, however, the separate pieces combine to form a coherent design that has a pattern and a unity of its own. The whole is more than the pieces that make it up. The question that faces schools as they respond to the demands for more choice and variety is how far they can go without abandoning some sort of experience that all students share as they grow into adult citizens.

This question becomes especially acute when the demand for choice moves outside the public school system, as, for instance, in the form of charter schools and voucher systems or of more public funding for private schools.

CHARTER SCHOOLS

CHARTER SCHOOLS COME IN many forms, but their central idea is straightforward enough. A charter school is a school run by a group of citizens who have asked for and received a charter from a ministry of education giving them the right to form their own school, with full public funding, provided it meets whatever conditions government sets. Such schools have been established in several American states, but in Canada they exist only in Alberta, though some other provinces are considering them. They are much favoured by critics of the public school system, who see them as a way to use tax dollars to get the kind of education they want for their children.

The charter itself can come in either a "weak" or a "strong" form. A weak charter allows a school to do almost anything it wants with a minimum of government supervision or regulation. A strong charter imposes stricter conditions, which usually include a commitment to follow the official curriculum, to accept all kinds of students regardless of background, and to open the school's accounts and procedures to official inspection. In either form, a charter spells out what a charter school can and cannot do. In a sense, it is a licence to operate.

Unless prevented by the terms of their charters, and these vary from place to place, charter schools are free to do much as they please. They can use whatever teaching methods they want. They can impose whatever disciplinary rules they like, within the law. They can hire whatever teachers they choose, qualified or unqualified, unionized or not. They are therefore not necessarily bound by union contracts concerning salaries or working conditions. If their charter permits, they can define their own target group, say, high academic achievers, second-language students or inner-city students. They can organize themselves as they see fit. A charter school can be rigidly traditionalist or radically innovative, or any shade in between, although most such schools so far are traditionalist, having been created by parents and sometimes teachers who see the public schools as too easygoing and permissive.

If the terms of their charters allow it, charter schools can be operated as for-profit businesses. In the United States, a number of companies now exist that operate schools in this way, and some entrepreneurs see schooling as ripe for private, for-profit investment, especially as public funding of education is cut back. They argue that their emphasis on profit ensures that their schools will be effective and efficient because otherwise they would not stay in business, and that competition among schools will ensure educational success.

Their critics worry that this concern for profit will lead charter schools to sacrifice the educational needs of students, or perhaps to take only those students whose education will be cheap and easy. At a deeper philosophical level, the critics of charter schools object to education being turned into a for-profit private business rather than a public service. One opponent of charter schools has this to say:

> Once the public discovers that it no longer has any meaningful role in determining what schools are for, it will quickly begin to wonder why it should be taxed to underwrite educating other people's children. Charter schools not only short-circuit our collective right to have a say in what schools should try to accomplish, but reinforce privatization's assumption that pleasing today's customers is the same as serving society's long-term interests."[1]

Supporters of charter schools see them as more democratic than the public school system, since they give parents and students a greater voice in shaping education as they see fit, cut through bureaucracy and make it possible for almost any group to organize its own schools. They also argue that their schools will be more effective than the public schools, since by their very nature they appeal to people who share certain beliefs and values and who are committed to their success. They believe that their schools will force the public schools to improve, since their very existence will give public schools competition. If, for example, a charter school is successful, it will attract students away from the public schools at no extra cost to parents, and so the public schools will have to shape up if they wish to survive. Moreover, say charter school supporters, their schools will not be a threat to social unity since they have to follow the provincial curriculum and generally meet official provincial requirements.

These arguments have not convinced the supporters of the public schools, who see charter schools as a threat to the survival of the public school system. Since charter schools are financed from within the existing education budget, every tax dollar that goes to them is a dollar that would otherwise have gone to the public school system. If charter schools were to become popular, the public schools would become poorer, until at some point the quality of education they offer would begin to suffer. If this were to happen, say public school supporters, parents who could afford to do so would probably feel forced to take their children out of the public schools, leaving them with only students whose parents are not able to send them elsewhere or whom charter schools refuse to accept because they are seen as too difficult to educate. The result would be a two-tier school system, with charter schools catering to the academically ambitious and public schools left to deal with everybody else, along the lines of the split between private and public hospitals in the United States. In addition, public school supporters worry that the very parents who are most concerned for their children and who work closely with schools might be attracted by charter schools, so that the public school system could lose a powerful support group.

Charter school supporters claim that their schools are not a threat to social unity, but public school supporters are not convinced. Charter schools in Alberta are currently required to follow provincial curricula, but there is no guarantee that this will always be so. There is a possibility that charter schools might appeal to distinct groups within a society—groups of different religion, race, social class or ethnic background—whether they intend it or not. For example, if a particular ethnic group opens a school, even though its doors are open to everyone, other groups might not attend it precisely because it is identified with the group that founded it. Similarly, if charter schools charge fees, whether directly or in the form of charges for computers and other equipment, or if students are responsible for their own transportation costs, then those who cannot afford it will be automatically excluded. There are, after all, many ways, both direct and indirect, in which schools can attract

certain kinds of students while putting others off. In the eyes of public school supporters, the public school's contribution to social unity
is too important to be put at risk. And in any case, they add, the public school system is open enough and flexible enough to accommodate everyone's wishes. If the public schools need improvement,
then the priority is to concentrate on improving them, not to abandon them and write them off as hopeless.

Needless to say, charter school supporters are not convinced by
these arguments, which they often dismiss as the rationalizations of
special interest groups, notably teachers' unions, teachers and school
trustees, whose careers are tied up with the public school system.
For their part, public school supporters say the real agenda of the
charter school people is to destroy, or at least to seriously weaken,
the public system, as part of a wider campaign to roll back the powers of government generally. And it is certainly true that charter
schools have attracted the support of neoconservative private enter-
prisers who identify government as a problem and see privatization
as the wave of the future.

The debate over charter schools is only in part about education.
It raises the broader question of the relationship between private profit
and public service, which we now see being debated in health care, the
contracting out of government work and privatization generally.

VOUCHERS

THOUGH THEY HAVE NOT been used in practice, vouchers are frequently held up as the cure for what critics believe is wrong with the
schools. They rest on two straightforward ideas. First, parents
would receive for each of their school-age children a voucher equivalent to what it would cost to educate one student at a particular
grade level for one year. Second, they would be free to use these
vouchers to educate their children in any way they saw fit, within
whatever regulations a ministry of education might enforce.

Vouchers could be used to choose among schools within the
public system, but in their purest form they might mean the end of
the public school system altogether. In its place would be a free market of schools that would offer their wares and attract parents and
students in any way they could. Schooling would no longer be a government monopoly, but a buyer's market. Education would become
a business, no different from hairdressing or auto repair. As with

most kinds of private business, there would still be government regulation and inspection to protect the consumer, but otherwise schools would be privatized.

The arguments for this root-and-branch approach to school reform are the same as those used to support charter schools. Indeed, opponents of charter schools see them as the Trojan horse that will lead to the introduction of full-blown voucher systems. Like charter schools, the supporters of vouchers see them as making schools more responsive to their parents and students, less bureaucratic and more efficient, while also creating a much greater range of choice. They see vouchers as both more effective and more democratic than the way we now run schools, though their critics point out that the administration of a voucher system would probably require a complicated bureaucracy, just as pensions and family allowances do.

Opponents of vouchers see them as a disaster waiting to happen. In their view, whatever one thinks of the quality of public schools, they are absolutely necessary for the existence of a civilized democracy. It is through public schools that students learn to accept difference and diversity, to work and play with people different from themselves, to learn the values and knowledge that hold a country together, and to grow up to become citizens. Public school supporters see this task of the schools as crucial, especially in a country as varied and divided as Canada. As they see it, the education of school-age children cannot be a purely private matter to be decided only by parents and students and for-profit entrepreneurs. Rather, it is a public affair, of interest to everyone, since the future of a country depends in large part on how its children are educated. Vouchers, therefore, it is argued, are not just a threat to the public school system, they are a threat to the existence of Canada itself.

Put in these terms, the argument sounds unnecessarily dramatic. But it has so far prevented vouchers from being seen as a practical path to educational reform in Canada.

PRIVATE SCHOOLS

APART FROM THE CHOICES that exist within the public school system, parents have always been able to go outside it and send their children to private schools, provided they are willing to pay the necessary fees. If they choose to do this, however, they still have to pay school taxes for the support of the public school system, and this has led some private school parents to complain that they are being taxed twice. Private schools do get some public funding, with the amount varying from province to province, so that arguments occur over the level of funding that should be given. Should private schools, for example, receive the full amount that public schools receive, or only some percentage of it, and if the latter, how much? In addition, if parents choose to pay private school fees, should they also have to pay school taxes to support a public school system they do not use?

These questions become even more complicated because of the existence of separate schools. These are not private schools, but religious-based schools that exist as part of the public school system in some provinces and are supported by school taxes and public funds, as in the case of Roman Catholic schools in Ontario, Saskatchewan and Alberta. Their origins are rooted in Canadian history and they are protected by constitutional guarantees dating back to 1867, which is why both Quebec's recent switch from Catholic and Protestant to French- and English-language boards, and Newfoundland's move from religious schools to a non-religious system, required an amendment to the Constitution that had to be approved by the federal Parliament. Despite this constitutional protection, however, the existence of publicly funded separate schools has led some other religious groups to claim that they deserve a similar status. Why, they ask, in a country that is committed to multiculturalism, should certain Christian schools be privileged in this way? Why should other religions not be given such rights? And if religious schools are supported by public funds why should non-religious private schools be excluded?

Private schools come in many shapes and sizes, but in very general terms they can be divided into three types. One type consists of those schools with a reputation for high academic achievement. Rightly or wrongly they are often described as elite schools, since they attract students mostly from wealthy backgrounds and charge high fees. A second type consists of small experimental or alternative schools, catering to parents and students who, for whatever reason, find the public schools too rigid. A third type, and one that has been growing in recent years, consists of schools that follow particular religious beliefs, mostly evangelical Christian, but also Jewish, Islamic and others.

The arguments surrounding private schools' claims to higher levels of public funding are much the same as those surrounding charter schools. Their supporters argue that parents should have the right to decide their children's education without having to pay extra for it; that private schools are at least as good and sometimes better than public schools; that they are doing the job of the public schools in educating children, thereby saving the public system money, and should therefore be funded for it; that they provide choice and variety in the school system; and that they are not really "private," since they have to follow provincial curricula, employ properly certificated teachers and stick to provincial rules and regulations. For this reason, they argue, they should be seen, not as "private," but as "independent," schools.

Their critics do not dispute their right to exist, but oppose their being publicly funded. As the critics see it, every dollar of public money that goes into private schools is a dollar less for the public schools and a threat to the quality of education that public schools can provide. Free public schools exist, say these critics, and if parents do not choose to use them, they should still have to support them. All taxpayers pay school taxes whether or not they have children in school, since schools are seen as benefitting everyone in society. Critics of private schools sometimes complain of their elitism, meaning that they appeal mostly to the wealthy who can afford to pay for their children's education, but this argument does not apply to the many private schools, mostly of a religious nature, whose fees are reasonably low.

All of the arguments for and against the public funding of private schools arise from one fundamental question: To what extent does Canadian democracy depend on its citizens having shared a more or less common education? If it does to any considerable extent, then the public school system deserves protection. If it does not, then it does not much matter what children learn. To put it another way: Is education a public trust or a private choice, and if it is something of both, where do we strike a balance? The belief that the public school system is one of the foundations of Canadian society, that it benefits everyone by educating children to become useful citizens and workers, and therefore must be protected at all costs, lies at the basis of all the arguments used against public funding of private schools.

HOME SCHOOLING

EDUCATING CHILDREN AT HOME is the most fundamental form of school choice. All provinces and territories allow this, provided that the quality of education at home is equal to that provided at school. In practice, this means that parents must follow the provincial curriculum and textbooks, see that their children write all provincial tests and examinations, and allow provincial officials to check on what and how they are teaching their children.

Parents choose home schooling for different reasons. Some want a particular religious or moral atmosphere that the public school cannot provide. Some think that public schools are too big to pay proper attention to students, or that their standards are too low, or that they are not creative enough. Some are unhappy with their local school. Some have ideas about education that differ from what their local school does, for example, in the choice of teaching methods or in the way the curriculum is organized. Some think the public school system is too permissive and liberal; some think it is is too strict and rigid.

In all cases, parents who choose home schooling obviously believe they can do a better job with their children than schools can, and that their children will both be happier and learn more at home. And, in any particular case, they could well be right. Whether home schooling is better or worse than public schooling depends entirely on circumstances. Parents usually are not as trained or qualified as teachers in particular subjects, and this might mean that children who are taught at home will not get the teaching they need in certain subjects and will not have access to workshops and laboratories. This presumably is why home schooling is more popular in the lower than in the higher grades. And children who are taught at home will obviously not experience the rough and tumble of mixing with a wide variety of other children in school. However, as supporters of home schooling point out, children who are taught at home can still mix with other children through sports programs and community activities.

As things stand, there is no evidence that children who are taught at home would have been any better off if they had been sent to school. They could be worse off if the reason parents kept them home was that they were not doing well at school in the first place. Provided that parents can match the academic demands of the school, while also meeting the social needs of children, there is no reason to believe that home schooling is inferior. It will never be the choice of more than a small minority of parents. And when both parents have to work outside the home, which, whether they want to or not, is the case in the majority of families these days, home schooling is an impossibility. Home schooling should be judged on its merits in any particular case. The question to ask is: Will it be better for this particular child in this particular situation? If the answer is yes, it is difficult to oppose it.

A VOICE FOR PARENTS

IT IS NO SECRET THAT children's education benefits when teachers and parents work together and most schools try to keep parents informed about what they are doing, at a minimum through parents' nights and report cards, but also through newsletters, visits, involving parents as volunteers in school activities and so on. In the past most such activities, however, have involved the schools informing parents, rather than vice versa. The communication has been one-way rather than two. Even when home-and-school associations exist, as they do in many elementary schools, they usually concentrate on helping the school through bake sales, teas, fund-raising and similar activities. What has been missing until recently is any way for parents to tell the schools what they want or expect. Individual parents take the initiative when they feel strongly enough, and schools insist that their doors are always open to parents, but there has been no organized way for parents to tell their schools what they would like them to do.

In recent years, many schools have emphasized the value of teachers and parents working together and sharing their ideas for the benefit of children. Increasingly, for example, teachers now contact all parents on a regular basis, either through home visits or by telephone, not only to tell them about school activities but also to get their advice on what their children need. Parent nights increasingly take the form of three-way consultations between teachers, parents and students, with displays of work, reports on progress and requests for ideas and suggestions. Where they have time and opportunity, parents increasingly get involved in school activities, for example, taking part in in-service training days, observing lessons, working as teacher aides or volunteers.

Recent school-reform efforts have gone a stage further by

involving parents directly in the operation of schools, usually in the form of a parent council that has real powers, including the hiring of teachers, the setting of budgets, the shaping of curriculum, the evaluation of students and many other things that only a few years ago were seen as the exclusive responsibility of teachers. Some provinces, such as Quebec and Manitoba, have made school councils mandatory, but all provinces now encourage their formation. How well they work depends very much on local circumstances, notably the attitude of both the parents and the teachers who serve on the councils. When both groups are able and willing to work together, as is usually the case, things go well. When parents have an axe to grind or teachers are feeling especially defensive, problems can arise.

Schools report that parent councils have worked well. In fact, schools have often found them them to be a welcome source of support. Generally speaking, the more parents get to know their children's school, to understand the problems it faces and what it is doing to solve them, the more supportive they are of what it is doing. This probably explains why survey after survey has found that even when people criticize the schools in general, they usually make an exception for the school they know or their children attend. It is notable that the farther people are removed from the classroom, the more critical they are likely to be of schools; the closer they are, the more supportive they become. In this sense, parent councils are an asset to schools.

DO WE NEED SCHOOL BOARDS?

HISTORICALLY CANADIAN SCHOOLS HAVE been controlled by locally elected school boards. In the early years of public schooling these boards were usually very small, but as education became more complicated and expensive, and as more and more students stayed on into high school, these original small school boards were combined, with or without their co-operation, into larger units, which provided the larger numbers of students that schools needed if they were to offer a variety of programs, and the bigger tax base to support them.

School trustees have the power to levy local school taxes, which the municipal government must collect whether it agrees with them or not, to set overall policies governing what schools can and cannot do, to hire and fire teachers and to set salaries, but they have never been completely independent. From the beginning of the public school system, they have operated under the authority of their provincial governments. These governments control curricula, decide what qualifications and training teachers must have, set over-all provincial salary scales, set and mark provincial examinations, generally formulate policies that schools must follow—for example, special education or school attendance—and supervise the conduct of school boards. Perhaps most important of all, some of the money to support schools comes from provincial grants, with local taxes making up only a part of school funding. This gives provincial or territorial governments considerable power, even though provincial grants have been reduced in recent years. It also makes for some degree of equality across boards, which otherwise would have to depend totally on local taxes.

Although school boards can exercise only those powers that provincial governments give them, they have for many years been seen as part of the system of local government. They are sometimes attacked by municipal councils, especially when the councils have to collect school taxes with which they do not agree, and they some-times argue with provincial policies, but only recently has it been suggested that we do not need them at all.

The arguments for getting rid of school boards are easy enough to understand, though not nearly as convincing as their supporters suggest. At one level, the move to abolish school boards is part of a wider neoconservative attack on governments generally. At its extreme, this view believes that governments are by definition inefficient and that almost everything they do could be done better either by business or by volunteers. Thus, to get rid of school boards is to get rid of a layer of government, and therefore a taxing author-ity, that we do not need.

At a less ideological level, the argument is that school boards have lost most of their powers anyway. Curricula, examinations, standards, teacher training and salaries, and policies of all kinds are decided at the provincial level. Decisions about teaching methods, discipline, professional development and all such local school mat-ters are decided by the schools themselves. As a result, the argument goes, there is nothing left for school boards to do. All that is need-ed is a straight two-way communication between ministries of edu-cation and individual schools. As for the argument that school boards reflect community control and local democracy in action, the reality is that usually fewer than thirty percent of people vote in school board elections, and most people have no idea who their school trustees are or what they stand for, or for that matter what school boards actually do once elected.

The logic of these arguments is that school boards should simply be eliminated, but only New Brunswick has gone this far. Manitoba considered reducing the number of its school boards, but has taken no action beyond encouraging voluntary mergers. Alberta and Ontario have reduced the numbers of their local boards by about half, while also taking away some of their powers, on the grounds that this will make for greater efficiency and greater economy. This seems unlikely, however, if only because many of these new boards now cover such large areas that it is difficult to see how they can do anything useful for the schools under their control. If nothing else, the old boards reflected their local communities. The new boards often straddle real community boundaries and in many cases their areas are little more than lines on the map. It might well be that they will become even more irrelevant than their critics now say they are.

There seems to be a fundamental contradiction in the argument of those who see getting rid of school boards as one more step in the downsizing of government, since, by abolishing boards, more power is automatically given to provincial ministries of education. In effect, they are making government more powerful, not less. The key elements of current reform efforts include tightening control over provincial curricula, reintroducing provincial examinations, making teachers more accountable and generally trying to raise standards. Whether these things are worth doing or not, they certainly put more power in the hands of provincial ministries of education. Indeed, that is their intent.

Whatever their weaknesses, school boards at least provide a channel between the schools and the communities they serve, and the smaller the board, the more effective the channel. It is easier for a parent who cannot get satisfaction from a school to go to the local school board than to have to deal with the distant provincial ministry of education. More generally, to abolish school boards is to weaken the community. Parents are interested in the schools their children attend, but once school boards, and therefore school districts, are abolished no one will take an interest in the schools of the community, except perhaps to see them as a tax burden.

The opponents of school boards respond to this argument by claiming that abolishing boards will mean more local control, not less, since it will give more power to the local school. They plan to make schools more or less independent units, with control of their own budgets and with more local autonomy, albeit within the framework of provincial rules and regulations. Principals will become more like managers and less like educators, which is why some provinces in recent years have told school principals that they can no longer belong to teachers' unions. It has even been suggested that schools might be better run by people with a business, not an education, background. Schools will be held accountable for achieving results, in terms of examination rates and so on, but they will also be freer than ever before to decide how to do it. The term that is used to describe all this is "site-based management;" it became popular in the 1980s, but there is no evidence that it has made much difference to schools, even when it was taken seriously.

Despite the talk of giving schools more responsibility, in practice schools find themselves with less freedom, not more, as they have to follow provincial curricula more closely, to prepare students for provincial tests and examinations that they have no voice in setting, and find their reputation judged on published comparisons of their students' test scores. At the same time, they find themselves deprived of the special services that their boards once offered, for instance, in terms of advice and professional development in various areas of the curriculum, in teaching methods and in special education—advice that was tailored to the particular needs of the school.

Equally important, a single school on its own will find it difficult to challenge provincial policy. Formerly a school could use its school board, which had more resources and influence, to gain support, to help make its case to other schools and to the community. Once school boards are abolished, however, schools will find themselves increasingly on their own. Provincial decisions to eliminate or reduce the numbers of school boards will do nothing to improve the quality of education and might well make it worse.

REFERENCES

1. Heather-Jane Robertson. *No More Teachers, No More Books.* Toronto: McClelland & Stewart, 1998, pp. 256-7.

CHAPTER THIRTEEN

School Reform

EFFECTIVE SCHOOLS

A GOOD TEACHER CAN EXIST in a bad school, but he or she will be much more effective in a good one. For a school not only affects children, but the teachers who staff it. It can make their work enjoyable or it can make it a daily experience of frustration. A good school creates a set of expectations, a standard of work and conduct, which shape both teachers and students. Students look forward to going to it. Teachers look forward to teaching in it. And parents are happy to send their children to it.

We have always known in a common-sense way that some schools are better than others, but for many years educational researchers believed this was due, not so much to anything schools did, but to the kinds of children who attended them. They thought that the most important influence on children's lives was the home environment and that schools could not compete with the influence of the home. Middle-class suburban schools send more children to university than do inner-city schools, not because of anything their teachers do, but because their students have many advantages, ranging from more private study space at home, through greater access to books and computers, to more money at their disposal and parents who have themselves been to university. In this view the secret to getting a good education was to choose your parents wisely and get yourself born into the middle class. In the words of a British sociologist, Basil Bernstein, schools cannot compensate for society.

However, there is plenty of evidence that schools can make a difference in students' lives, and researchers realized that some schools were indeed more successful than others, regardless of the kinds of students who went to them, the districts in which they were located or the income level of parents. Even in poverty-stricken inner-city areas, where schools often faced major social problems, some schools were more successful than others. They had lower dropout rates and better attendance records; their students got better marks and were more likely to go on to decent jobs or to college or university; discipline was better; students, teachers and parents were happier; and in just about every imaginable way they worked more smoothly, even though their students were no different from those who went to less successful schools. In the language of the researchers, some schools were more "effective" than others.

The search for effective schools became a major theme in educational research in the 1970s and 1980s, and researchers soon identified the characteristics that effective schools shared. They are:

- a sense of common purpose that is shared by teachers, students and parents
- a high level of commitment by teachers and students in all aspects of school life
- an emphasis on clear academic goals for all students and an assumption that all students can and will succeed academically at a reasonable level
- teachers who share a common philosophy and see themselves as colleagues working for a common purpose
- well-organized lessons that focus on academic learning
- an approach to discipline that is firm but fair and makes sense to students
- a principal who takes an active interest in teaching and learning, works with teachers as colleagues, but also takes final responsibility for running the school
- good working relationships with parents and the community in general

The researchers decided that the most important characteristic that effective schools have in common is the overall climate and atmosphere of the school. Effective schools are driven by a shared set of beliefs as to what education is all about, and, more specifically, what they intend to do for their students. They see a philosophy of education not as something to be dusted off on ceremonial occasions and then forgotten, but rather as something to be used to direct everything they do, from organizing the curriculum, through teaching and evaluating students, to setting up discipline and reporting policies, and everything else that is involved in the school's operation. Moreover, this philosophy is not dreamed up in the principal's office; it is worked out by the teachers and used to guide and evaluate everything the school does. When new teachers are hired, they are hired not simply because they are qualified professionals, but because they are willing to work within the philosophy of the school. Equally important, this philosophy is shared with parents and with students. When students have to be disciplined or brought up to speed, it is done in terms of the school's philosophy, so that the students themselves see that it is taken seriously and that ignoring it carries consequences.

A shared philosophy is only one part of the picture. A lot also depends on what the philosophy is. In the case of effective schools, a crucial element is the belief that academic knowledge and skills are important for everyone and that all students can and will succeed, regardless of family circumstances, personal difficulties, social class, race, gender or any other condition. Teachers in effective schools set high expectations for all students and do everything they can to hold students to them. They do so, however, in ways that are sensitive to the lives of students. To have high expectations does not mean failing half the class because they do not measure up. It means digging to find out why students fail and what can be done about it. If they do not take their work seriously, that is one thing. But if there are other reasons, for example, health or personal problems, inappropriate teaching, or students' failure to understand what they have been taught, that is something very different, and teachers then set about to correct whatever it is. Above all, it means not writing off students or accepting a lower standard of work because they are thought to be non-academic, low-ability or unmotivated.

In a way this all sounds very trite, but it can have profound consequences on the ways schools operate. No one is saying that simply telling students that we expect them to do well will work miracles. Few students respond to this kind of feel-good fakery—but they do respond to teachers who take a genuine interest in their well-being. What the research says is that expecting all students to do well can involve rethinking how we teach and how we run our schools. For example, most schools are the slaves of their timetable. Students either successfully complete their course in the time allotted or they do not, even though they learn in different ways at different speeds. Until we make the timetable flexible enough to accommodate different rates of learning, we inevitably condemn some students to failure. To set high expectations for all students carries with it the obligation to set up conditions that make it possible for them to meet those expectations.

Students are more likely to do well when their teachers know them well enough to detect potential problems, to gain their trust and confidence, to encourage and challenge them, and when needed to discipline them without losing their respect. This means that teachers must be able to get to know their students thoroughly and ensure that no student is neglected or overlooked.

The most obvious way to do this is to make sure schools and classes do not become so big that students get lost in the crowd. Some researchers are suggesting these days that no school should take more than about eight hundred or so students. Where schools are bigger than this, they can be broken down to schools within the school, each holding two or three hundred students and working more or less as independent units, so that they can create a sense of belonging and commitment among their students and build close links between students and teachers. Schools are increasingly using advisory groups, whereby throughout their school life fifteen or so students meet regularly with a teacher-adviser, who gets to know them well and serves as a source of advice, help and support when they need it. Another approach, found mostly at the middle years/junior high level, but increasingly in high schools too, is to create teaching teams of three or four teachers, each a specialist in a particular subject, but sharing responsibility for ninety or a hundred students and planning their own teaching timetable so that they can organize teaching as they see fit. In this way, teachers can work together, get to know their students more closely and combine the academic and advisory duties that are central to good teaching. A less ambitious approach, recommended by the Radwanski inquiry into school dropouts in Ontario in 1987, is for teachers to teach two subjects to the same group of students, and so get to know them better. Whatever approach is chosen, the aim is the same: to find a way for every student in a school to be known well by at least one teacher and to make sure that all students have at least one teacher they trust enough to turn to when they face a problem.

Working closely with students in this way also involves working with parents, and another characteristic of effective schools is that they establish close links with parents and the community at large. To a large extent, this is a matter of communication. Effective schools make sure that parents know what they are doing and why— not just when things go wrong or when a student is in trouble, but as a matter of routine. Often teachers visit or phone all their students' parents at regular intervals. In addition, parents are usually involved in the school, whether as volunteers, teacher aides or as members of the school council. However it is done, effective schools operate with the support and goodwill of parents, largely because they maintain regular contact with them, take the trouble to explain what they are doing, listen openly to parents' suggestions, ideas and criticisms, and make it crystal clear that they want to work with them for the benefit of their children.

Research shows, however, that what makes schools effective is not any particular list of characteristics but a shared spirit of commitment. It is not so much what schools do or do not do, but the state of mind in which they work. Effective schools come in many shapes. Some are traditional, some experimental. Some are urban, others suburban or rural. Some are big, others small. There is no one master blueprint. Instead there is a common commitment, shared by all the teachers involved, working together with principals, who see themselves as teachers rather than managers or administrators. Researchers call it the "ethos" of the school. And this is what makes it so difficult to figure out how a school becomes effective in the first place. Simply drawing up a list of characteristics and ordering schools to adopt them does not work, though this has not stopped some administrators from trying. Sometimes a principal is the catalyst, sometimes a group of teachers, more often a combination of principals and teachers working together in a collaborative effort, but there is no single formula to fit each and every occasion.

SCHOOL-BUSINESS PARTNERSHIPS

SOME OF TODAY'S SCHOOL reformers are also suggesting that business should be involved in running schools. Business is certainly taking an active interest in schools these days. Many employers expect the schools to produce graduates with the skills and knowledge they will need in the workplace and have been very critical of what they see as their weaknesses in this regard. They have also been active in promoting the argument that the failings of the schools have left Canada unprepared for the demands of the new global economy and that school reform is an important element of success in world markets. Business in Canada has energetically pushed for certain kinds of school reform: raising standards in mathematics and science, improving literacy levels, increasing computer skills, teaching good work habits and making both teachers and students more supportive of business generally.

Across the country, provincial ministries of education have accepted business criticisms of the schools and have reshaped curricula in line with business priorities, placing more emphasis on job training, technology, mathematics and science, and the needs of the economy, even at the expense of such traditional goals as citizenship and personal development.

School-business partnerships have become an important element of school reform. These partnerships come in many forms, but they share some common characteristics. They usually involve business supplying equipment and resources, and sometimes direct funding, to the schools. They often feature some kind of staff exchange, with teachers spending time in business and business people working in the schools. They usually require students to learn business-related skills and knowledge and to get relevant job experience as part of their school program. These kinds of partnerships exist most often in high school technical and vocational programs, but they are also found in academic areas and can reach down into the elementary school grades.

In addition, business is involved with schools in other ways. Some companies, for example, sponsor projects in general education, as in the case of an elementary-grades reading program in which teachers reward successful students with a particular company's pizza coupons. Some companies produce curriculum materials that contain useful information, for instance, about forestry, or atomic energy and conservation, but also present arguments that support particular positions their industry favours. Companies for many years have looked for ways to get their company logos into schools, whether on book covers, atlases, scoreboards or through some other method. A new development of this kind is the appearance in some schools of plaques or notices, featuring a company logo and acknowledging a gift of equipment, often computer-related, or some other kind of support.

Some businesses now see in schools an opportunity for making money. Probably the best known is the television service created by an American entrepreneur, Chris Whittle, consisting of a daily twelve-minute broadcast that comprises nine minutes of news and three minutes of commercials. Schools that sign up for the service must guarantee that ninety percent of their students will watch it daily and in return get a free satellite dish and television monitors. The profit for the company comes from charging advertising fees, but critics of the project object to turning schoolchildren into a captive audience for advertisers. Even so, roughly half of American schools have signed up for the service, though it has made very little headway in Canada. The same entrepreneur, Chris Whittle, has also set up Project Edison, which in effect offers to take over the operation of schools, either in whole or in part, for a fee, and promises to do a better job than the schools themselves. So far, only two U.S. school systems, Baltimore and Hartford, have actually contracted out their schools to private firms, and in both cases with unsatisfactory results, but the idea of contracting out education is now alive and well.

None of this amounts to direct control of schooling. No one in Canada has yet gone as far as the Thatcher government did in England when it required school councils to include members of their local business communities. Nor has anyone in Canada yet contracted out academic school services, though food and soft drink manufacturers have signed contracts with school boards and universities that give them exclusive advertising and sales rights, as in the case of Coca-Cola at the University of British Columbia and Pepsi-Cola with the Toronto School Board. School people are divided on the question of whether, or to what extent, to co-operate with business.

In some ways, this co-operation goes back a long way. For example, newspapers have for many years operated news-in-the-classroom programs. Industries have long sponsored teaching materials, teacher in-services and student field trips. The Chamber of Commerce has long operated its Junior Achievement program, where students learn the dos and don'ts of business life. What is new today is the scale and intensity of business-school links. In times of cutbacks and downsizing, it is not all that difficult for business to make schools offers that they cannot afford to refuse. In 1994 the Toronto Schools Board earned one million dollars from its contract with Pepsi-Cola, and around the country schools and school boards are making money from selling advertising in school buses, on computer screen savers, on gymnasium scoreboards and other such devices.

TWO KINDS OF SCHOOL REFORM

Two APPROACHES TO SCHOOL reform have emerged in recent years. One is associated most closely with provincial governments and ministries of education, and is centralist in its orientation. It takes the form of centrally imposed, province-wide rules and regulations that all schools have to follow. It is based on the belief that schools have had too much independence and that what we need now is more consistency and uniformity throughout the school system. Schools are to follow provincial curricula much more closely than they have in the past. In turn, provincial curricula are to be made academically tougher and backed up with province-wide examinations, while schools' success or failure is to be judged by their students' examination results, often made public so that parents can decide which schools are good and which are bad. This combination of central control, parent choice and teacher accountability will, we are told, raise standards and improve the overall quality of education.

The other approach is very different. It can be described as localist, since its supporters see the key to reform, not in centralized regulations, but in changes in the way schools operate at the local level. This is why, for example, the Gordon Foundation is supporting efforts by Canadian schools to implement reforms on a school-by-school basis. Localists do not believe that centrally imposed rules and regulations will be effective. Indeed, they fear that they might cramp the style of good schools while doing nothing for schools that are not as good. Localists point out that schools are not like a hockey team where the players are supposed to follow the instructions of their coach. Nor do they not operate like the military where orders are issued by headquarters and carried out by local units. Nor are they like businesses where instructions are sent out by head office and obeyed by local branches. Even in sports, in the military and in business, this simple top-down process rarely operates smoothly. Hockey players have been known to ignore their coaches, and even in the military, which supposedly runs on discipline and command, resourceful units can find a thousand ways to get around their orders or shape them to their satisfaction.

Schools are much more complicated. They do not have clear lines of command. They have to answer to parents, to the local community and to their local school board, as well as to the provincial ministry of education. They have to take into account the nature and needs of their students. In addition, teachers expect a certain amount of professional freedom in deciding how best to do their job. And people can and do honestly disagree on just what their job ought to be. In other words, schools are complex organizations that are not easily changed from the outside. Indeed, attempts to change them from the outside can easily backfire if teachers do not agree with what they are being told to do. With this in mind, localists believe that successful change can come only from within the schools themselves. This approach to school reform will obviously be a lot messier than any neat package of province-wide regulations and policies all wrapped up and nicely printed, but it will, say the localists, be much more effective.

The most sensible approach might be to find the most appropriate combination of the two approaches. Local change affects only the local school level and has little or no effect on the school system as a whole, except by force of example. It might not even work at the local school level if the school board or ministry of education is not supportive. Similarly, centralized change will be no change at all if local schools decide to resist or sabotage it.

Although the centralists dominate the ministries of education and have caught the attention of the media, the localists have had the most positive impact on schools. Among the best known are Theodore Sizer, Henry Levin, Deborah Meier and James Comer. All four are Americans but they have had some influence in Canada and certainly show what is possible.

Sizer's "essential schools" are small high schools or schools within schools, with a curriculum pared down to central academic priorities (Less is More is one of Sizer's mottos), with a good deal of curricular flexibility and with patterns of teaching that require teachers and students to work collaboratively over long periods of time. Levin's "accelerated schools" offer at-risk elementary-grades students the same kind of program and teaching that is usually restricted to so-called gifted students, with enriched curricula and challenging assignments, and with a high level of parental involvement. Meier has gained an international reputation for her work in an inner-city New York high school that by any normal consideration should have been swamped by the problems it faced, but instead achieved a consistently high degree of academic success through treating curriculum flexibly, using a wide variety of teaching and learning approaches and being always prepared to rethink what it does. Comer's program works with young inner-city children in ways that demand close co-operation among teachers, parents and resource people, adapting curricula to the circumstances of children but without compromising academic standards. All four programs, and there are many others like them, are making a substantial contribution to school reform, but by following a localist, not a centralist approach. In fact, they consciously avoid the two serious weaknesses of the centralist approach: its ignoring of history and its oversimplification.

The centralists' ignoring of history is surprising in view of their general belief that we did things better in the past and that the key to school reform is to get back to the basics, which we allegedly abandoned in our fascination with child-centred, progressive education. When we look back to the past, however, we find not a golden age of strong discipline, high standards and academic achievement, but the same problems and the same complaints.

In 1968 a major investigation of history teaching across the country, A.B. Hodgetts's *What Culture? What Heritage?* was scathing in its criticisms. Curricula were outdated, textbooks were awful, and the quality of teaching was even worse. As a result, students not only did not know their history, they hated it. And the report emphasized that this was no new development. Rather, it was the result of more than thirty years of neglect and poor teaching.

Throughout the 1950s and 1960s there was a constant barrage of criticism to the effect that schools were not doing their job. In 1953, a University of Manitoba professor, Joseph Katz, criticized high school history programs, finding that they and their teachers presented students with a dried-out version of history, stripped of any semblance of interest or excitement. Katz's report was a model of tact, however, compared to what university academics were saying at the time. In submissions to the 1950 Massey Royal Commission on the Arts in Canada, they took dead aim at the high schools. According to the eminent sociologist, S.D. Clark, high school graduates were inadequately trained in language, mathematics and history. The head of the English department at Queen's University said that they could neither spell nor write a simple sentence correctly. He estimated that up to a quarter of university students could not write acceptable English. The University of Saskatchewan historian, Hilda Neatby, was even more dismissive of the schools, saying that students could not read, write or think.

These criticisms were voiced in the early 1950s, but they looked back to the schools of the 1940s. This was the period when we are now led to believe that the basics were supposed to be alive and well, when standards were high and when the quality of education was rigorously controlled by province-wide curricula and provincial examinations. Things were no better in the 1930s, though people were too busy surviving the depression to worry too much about what was going on in the schools. Nonetheless, in 1935 a visiting expert surveyed Canadian schools and declared that they imposed on students "a severe demand for sheer laboriousness" but demanded little in the way of "genuine, spontaneous intellectual effort."[1]

It would not be difficult to compile a long list of such criticisms. The point is obvious. There never was a golden age of education, which we have somehow abandoned. Centralist reformers want to bring back many of the practices of the past, but they ignore the fact that, in their day, these practices were themselves often much criticized.

The centralist approach to school reform oversimplifies a very complex problem. It is based on the belief that the solution to the schools' problems is to be found within the school system itself. More examinations, a tighter curriculum, different teaching methods— these and other such measures will improve the quality of our schools. However, this ignores all the realities that in recent years have turned the schools into social agencies as much as educational institutions. Sex education, street-proofing, peer counselling, breakfast programs, AIDS education, sustainable development and many other activities taken on by schools are responses to pressing social problems that the schools did not create but are expected to solve. Even as I write these words in November 1998, Winnipeg school principals have been instructed that, due to cutbacks in school medical services, they are now responsible for checking students for head lice. It seems the easiest way to avoid having to deal with a social problem in Canada is to redefine it as a question of education and hand it over to the schools. As a result, the schools find themselves in a double bind: they cannot solve the problems, but in trying to do so, they have less time for their academic work and so find themselves under attack.

It is not especially surprising that teachers are suspicious of the centralist agenda. This does not surprise the centralists, of course. They largely blame teachers for the schools' problems anyway. Teachers are said to be part of the self-serving "education establishment" that caused the problems in the first place. There is no reason teachers should be any less interested in protecting themselves and their working conditions than anyone else, but the centralists are wrong to attack them. The research is clear: teachers define their success and their job satisfaction largely in terms of their impact on students. They work with students every working day. If they are not enthusiastic about the centralist approach to school reform, it is worth asking why. Any attempt to reform schools that ignores or insults the expertise of those who are expected to implement it is likely to run into problems.

The puzzle about school-reform efforts in Canada to date is why the centralist approach has attracted so much attention. It looks neater, no doubt, and it is certainly easier to issue a new curriculum guideline or to set a new examination than to work with real students in a real classroom. It offers apparently plausible solutions to the questions of concerned parents, although many parents seem to be reasonably happy with their local schools. It would be a pity, however, if the needed changes in our schools were decided in ignorance of the full range of the possibilities of reform.

REFERENCES

1. Fred Clarke. "Education in Canada—An Impression." *Queen's Quarterly*, XLII, Autumn, 1935, pp. 309-321.

SUGGESTIONS FOR FURTHER READING

Descriptions of Schools in Action

A good place to begin is with Ken Dryden's *Our Kids, Our Teachers, Our Classrooms* (Toronto: McClelland & Stewart, 1995), and Sandra Contenta's *Rituals of Failure: What Our Schools Really Teach* (Toronto: Between the Lines, 1993). In *Cries from the Corridor* (Toronto: Methuen, 1980), Peter McLaren describes his experience in a Toronto elementary school. Don Sawyer describes a year in a Newfoundland outport school in his *Tomorrow is School* (Vancouver, Douglas & McIntyre, 1979). Samuel Freedman's *Small Victories: The Real World of a High School Teacher* is a sympathetic account of teaching in a lively, American inner-city school which is also typical of Canadian experience. More scientific in its approach is John Goodlad's national survey of American schools, *A Place Called School* (New York: McGraw-Hill, 1984). Though American, its findings are applicable to the Canadian experience.

Critics of Schools

For the United States, see Edward D. Hirsch's *The Schools We Need and Why We Don't Have Them* (New York: Doubleday, 1996). For Canada, see Andrew Nikiforuk's *School's Out: The Catastrophe of Public Education and What We Can Do About It* (Toronto: McFarland, Walter & Ross, 1993), and the opening chapters of Peter C. Emberley and Walter R. Newell's *Bankrupt Education: The Decline of Liberal Education in Canada* (Toronto: University of Toronto Press, 1994). As these titles suggest, critics of the schools adopt a take-no-prisoners approach to public education. For an equally committed response to such critics see Maude Barlow and Heather-Jane Robertson's *Class Warfare: The Assault on Canada's Schools* (Toronto: Key Porter, 1994); and Heather-Jane Robertson's, *No More Teachers,*

No More Books: The Commercialization of Canada's Schools (Toronto: McClelland & Stewart, 1998). For an American response, applicable to Canada also, see David C. Berliner and Bruce J. Biddle's *Manufactured Crisis: Myths, Fraud, and the Attacks on America's Public Schools* (Reading, Mass.: Addison-Wesley, 1995).

The Goals of Education

This is a huge topic. One of the best ways to approach it is through Amélie Oksenberg Rorty (ed.)'s *Philosophers on Education: New Historical Perspectives* (London: Routledge, 1998). Also valuable, though one has to translate the American references into a Canadian context, is Neil Postman's *The End of Education: Redefining the Value of School* (New York: Knopf, 1995). A personal favourite of mine, though little known these days, is H.G. Wells's, *The Salvaging of Civilization: The Probable Future of Mankind* (New York: Macmillan, 1921). For the link between education and citizenship, see Derek B. Heater's *Citizenship: The Civic Ideal in World History, Politics, and Education* (London: Longmans, 1990).

The Curriculum

For descriptions of the historical background of Canadian schooling, see Paul Axelrod's *The Promise of Schooling: Education in Canada 1800-1914* (Toronto: University of Toronto Press, 1997) and Ronald Manzer's *Canadian Public School and Political Ideas: Canadian Educational Policy in Historical Perspective* (Toronto: University of Toronto Press, 1994). For the development of the Canadian curriculum, see George S. Tomkins' *A Common Countenance: Stability and Change in the Canadian Curriculum* (Toronto: Prentice-Hall, 1986). The classic account of how to design a curriculum is Ralph Tyler's *Basic Principles of Curriculum and Instruction* (Chicago: University of Chicago Press, 1949). For criticisms of the "Tyler model," see William Pinar (ed.)'s *Curriculum Theorizing: The Reconceptualists* (Berkeley: McCutchan, 1975). There have been many analyses of curricula as instruments of ideology; perhaps the most useful is Michael Apple's *Ideology and Curriculum* (New York: Routledge & Kegan Paul, 1979). On streaming and tracking, see Jeannie Oakes's *Keeping Track: How Schools Structure Inequality* (New Haven: Yale University Press, 1985). For a British example of how this works in practice, see Paul Willis's *Learning to Labour: How Working Class Kids Get Working Class Jobs* (Farnborough: Saxon House, 1976). For A Canadian application, see Bruce Curtis, David Livingstone and Harry Smaller's *Stacking the Deck: The Streaming of Working-class Kids in Ontario Schools* (Toronto: Lorimer, 1992).

Teachers and Teaching

On teachers and their lives, see Alan J. King and M.J. Peart's *Teachers in Canada* (Ottawa: Canadian Teachers Federation, 1992); Andy Hargreaves's *Changing Teachers, Changing Times: Teachers' Work and Culture in the Post-modern Age* (New York: Teachers College Press, 1994); and A. Lockhart's *Teachers in Canada* (Toronto: University of Toronto Press, 1991). On teaching, see Ken Osborne's, *Teaching for Democratic Citizenship* (Toronto: Lorimer, 1991); Herb Kohl's *Growing Minds: On Becoming a Teacher* (New York: Harper, 1984); Satu Repo's *Making Schools Matter: Good Teachers at Work* (Toronto: Lorimer, 1998); and Neil Postman and Charles Weingartner's *Teaching as a Subversive Activity* (New York: Dell, 1979). This last title should be read together with a later book by the same authors, *Teaching as a Conserving Activity*. Also worth pondering is Ira Shor and Paolo Freire's *A Pedagogy for Liberation* (South Hadley, Mass.: Bergin & Garvey, 1987).

Students and Learning

For a look at students' lives outside school, see Myrna Kostash's *No Kidding: Inside the World of Teenage Girls* (Toronto: McClelland & Stewart, 1987). See also *Growing Up In Canada: Longitudinal Survey of Children and Youth* (Ottawa: StatsCan, 1996). See also Maureen Baker (ed.)'s, *Families: Changing Trends in Canada* (Toronto: McGraw-Hill-Ryerson, 1996); John F. Conway's *The Canadian Family in Crisis* (Toronto: Lorimer, 1997) and Reginald W. Bibby and Donald C. Posterski's *The Emerging Generation: An Inside Look at Canada's Teenagers* (Toronto: Irwin, 1985). On childhood generally, see Neil Postman's *The Disappearance of Childhood* (New York: Dell, 1982); and David Elkind's *The Hurried Child: Growing Up Too Fast Too Soon* (Reading, Mass.: Addison-Wesley, 1988). For historical accounts of growing up in Canada, see Neil Sutherland's *Children in English-Canadian Society: Framing the Twentieth Century Consensus*

(Toronto: University of Toronto Press, 1976) and *Growing Up: Childhood in English Canada from the Great War to the Age of Television* (Toronto: University of Toronto Press, 1997); also see Doug Owram's *Born at the Right Time: A History of the Baby Boom Generation* (Toronto: University of Toronto Press, 1996). On the education of girls, see Jane Gaskell, Arlene McLaren and Myra Novogrodsky's *Claiming an Education: Feminism and Canadian Schools* (Toronto: Lorimer, 1989); and Myra and David Sadker's *Failing at Fairness: How American Schools Cheat Girls* (New York: Scribners, 1994). For the theory that girls and women have their own ways of learning, see Mary Field Belenky, Blythe McVicker Clinchy, Nancy Rule Goldberger and Jill Mattuck Tarule's *Women's Ways of Knowing: The Development of Self, Voice and Mind* (New York: Basic Books, 1986); and the same authors' *Knowledge, Difference and Power: Essays Inspired by Women's Ways of Knowing* (New York: Basic Books, 1996). On intelligence testing, see Stephen Jay Gould's *The Mismeasure of Man* (New York: Norton, 1981). On the idea that intelligence is multifaceted, see Robert J. Sternberg's *The Triarchic Mind: A New Theory of Human Intelligence* (New York: Penguin, 1988); and Howard Gardner's *Frames of Mind: The Theory of Multiple Intelligences* (New York: Basic Books, 1983). For examples of what Gardner's theory means in practice, see Howard Gardner (ed.)'s *Multiple Intelligences: The Theory in Practice, A Reader* (New York: Basic Books, 1993).

School Reform

A comprehensive examination of all aspects of school reform can be found in David T. Conley's *Roadmap to Restructuring: Charting the Course of Change in American Education* (Eugene, Oregon: Clearing House on Educational Management, 1997). A balanced approach to school reform can be found in Jeannie Oakes and Martin Lipton's *Making the Best of Schools* (New Haven: Yale University Press, 1992). See also Linda Darling-Hammond's *The Right to Learn: A Blueprint for Creating Schools that Work* (San Francisco: Jossey-Bass, 1997); John Goodlad's *Educational Renewal: Better Teachers, Better Schools* (San Francisco, Jossey-Bass, 1994); and Theodore R. Sizer's *Horace's School: Redesigning the American High School* (Boston: Houghton Mifflin, 1992). For an enthusiastic American endorsement of charter schools, see Joe Nathan's *Charter Schools: Creating Hope and Opportunity for American Education* (San Francisco: Jossey-Bass,

1996) For arguments against, see the article by Murray Dobbin "Charting a Course to Social Division: The Charter School Threat to Public Education in Canada" in *Our Schools, Ourselves*, April/May 1997, pp. 48-82. On the general idea of privatizing schools, see Joseph Murphy's *The Privatization of Schooling: Problems and Possibilities* (Berkley: Sage, 1996). For descriptions of school reform in action, see Deborah Meier's *The Power of their Ideas: Lessons from a Small School in Harlem* (Boston: Beacon Press, 1995); and Edward B. Fiske's *Smart Schools, Smart Kids: Why Do Some Schools Work?* (New York: Simon & Schuster, 1991). One of the few Canadian teachers who have offered a vision of education in the future is R.G. Des Dixon in *Future Schools: And How to Get There from Here* (Toronto: ECW Press, 1992).

Keeping Up To Date

The most practical way to keep up to date with what is going on in education is to read the journals and magazines. There are very few such magazines in Canada designed for a general readership. The most accessible are *Our Schools, Ourselves* (5502 Atlantic Street, Halifax B3H 9Z9); and *Education Canada* (Canadian Education Association, Suite 8-200, 2252 Bloor Street West, Toronto, M5S 1V5) Two American journals are also useful, since American developments often spill over into Canada. They are *Phi Delta Kappan* and *Educational Leadership*.

INDEX